# THE MYSTERY
# OF GOD
## *Who God Is and Why He Matters*

Dear Friends in Christ,

The *Mystery of God* Formation Program has been created by Word on Fire Catholic Ministries to help Christians better understand what the Church means by "God" and to encourage believers to grow closer to the Most Holy Trinity.

In these days of increasing secularization and more alarmingly, increasing and often strident atheism, every Christian needs to take the "God question" seriously. Although our knowledge of God here on earth will never be complete, the rich, intellectual tradition of the Church has a lot to say to illuminate and clarify what we mean when we say "God."

From the first apostles to St. Thomas Aquinas and beyond, the Church has developed a definite point of view about who God is and what he is not. Many times the atheists are arguing against a god that is not the one, true God of Christian belief. This program can help you better understand and explain the God who created the universe and sustains all life through an endless outpouring of his infinite love and mercy.

The film for the *Mystery of God* program was created on location at the beautiful campus of Mundelein Seminary and the study program was written under my direction by Trent Horn, apologist and author of *Answering Atheism: How to Make the Case for God with Logic and Charity*. It is my hope that *The Mystery of God: Who God Is and Why He Matters* will enrich your faith and draw you ever closer to the one who is ipsum esse, or "being itself," so you can confidently and boldy proclaim, "I believe in God the Father almighty, creator of heaven and earth. I believe in Jesus Christ, his only Son, our Lord and in the Holy Spirit."

Peace,

*Bishop Robert Barron*

Most Reverend Robert E. Barron
Auxiliary Bishop of Los Angeles
Founder of Word on Fire Catholic Ministries

# WORD on FIRE

5215 Old Orchard Road, Suite 410 · Skokie, IL · 60077 · www.WordOnFire.org · www.MysteryOfGod.com

*Bishop Robert Barron's*

# THE MYSTERY
## OF GOD

*Who God Is and Why He Matters*

A CATHOLIC STUDY PROGRAM presented by
**MOST REV. ROBERT E. BARRON**

STUDY GUIDE written by
**TRENT HORN**

WORD
on FIRE

www.WORDONFIRE.org

# THE MYSTERY
OF GOD

## TABLE OF CONTENTS

# THE MYSTERY
## OF GOD

WORD
on FIRE

# ATHEISM AND WHAT WE MEAN BY "GOD"

## LESSON ONE OUTLINE

I. INTRODUCTION
    A. Atheism and September 11

II. ATHEISM
    A. Definition of Atheism
    B. Strong vs. Weak Atheists
    C. Agnosticism

III. ARE WE ALL ATHEISTS?
    A. St. Anselm's Definition of God
    B. False Understandings of God
    C. "Moralistic Therapeutic Deism"

IV. WHAT IS GOD?
    A. Essence and Exsistence
    B. God as Being Itself

V. GOD MADE IN MAN'S IMAGE
    A. Ludwig Feuerbach
    B. Argument from Desire

VI. ATHEISTIC EXISTENTIALISM
    A. Karl Marx
    B. Jean Paul Sartre
    C. God and Freedom
    D. Objective Goodness

LESSON ONE

# ATHEISM AND WHAT WE MEAN BY "GOD"

Prior to September 11, 2001, atheists typically considered religion to be a generally harmless fiction, save for the actions of a few violent extremists. But after the events of that terrible day, many atheists came to believe that religion itself was dangerous since it could, allegedly, motivate good people to do terrible things in the name of blind faith. The 9/11 attacks encouraged atheists like Sam Harris and Richard Dawkins to write their bestselling diatribes against religion.

Dawkins hopefully opines in his 2006 book *The God Delusion*, "Imagine, with John Lennon, a world with no religion. Imagine no suicide bombers, no 9/11 . . . . If this book works as I intend, religious readers who open it will be atheists when they put it down."[1]

But as Proverbs 18:17 says, "He who states his case first seems right, until the other comes and examines him." The goal of these lessons is to equip you to better understand not only the arguments of atheists, but also the loving, triune God of the Catholic faith, and to share him with others in our skeptical world.

## ATHEISM

Atheism comes from the Greek word for "God" (*theos*) and the Greek word for "without" (a). Hence, an atheist is someone who is "without God" or, more specifically, an atheist is someone who is without belief in the existence of God. When you encounter people who identify as atheists there are two types you will probably meet:

**Strong atheists:** These aren't atheists who go to the gym a lot. Instead, a strong atheist is someone who makes this very strong claim: "God does not exist," or "There is no God." This is the traditional definition the *Catechism of the Catholic Church* refers to when it says that atheism "rejects or denies the existence of God" (CCC 2125). Of course, such a sweeping claim requires

very good evidence to support it, and because of this heavy burden of proof many atheists choose to adopt a "weaker" or less controversial position instead.

**Weak atheists:** Weak atheists are often skeptical of the claims strong atheists make. They may even agree with the Psalmist who said, "The fool says in his heart, 'There is no God'" (Ps 14:1).[2] He might say that he can't prove God does not exist, but he doesn't have to because weak atheists say they simply "lack a belief in God" or they are "without God" in their lives. They say the burden of proof is on the theist (person who believes God exists). If the theist can't make his case, then atheism wins by default.

However, atheists can't be defined merely by their lack of belief in God. Puppies, babies, and automobiles lack a belief in God, but that doesn't make your dog, your infant, or your pickup truck an atheist. Instead, a weak atheist is more properly defined as "someone who lacks a belief in God because he believes there are no good reasons to justify believing that God exists." But this definition already belongs to another person involved in the debate over God's existence—the agnostic.

Traditionally, in the history of philosophy, when it came to the question, "Does God exist?" a theist answered "Yes," an atheist answered "No," and an agnostic answered "I don't know." For an agnostic, the evidence is inconclusive in both directions. Pope Benedict XVI actually spoke positively of such people in a 2011 address:

> In addition to the two phenomena of religion and anti-religion, a further basic orientation is found in the growing world of agnosticism: people to whom the gift of faith has not been given, but who are nevertheless on the lookout for truth, searching for God. Such people do not simply assert: "There is no God." They suffer from his absence and yet are inwardly making their way towards him, inasmuch as they seek truth and goodness. They are "pilgrims of truth, pilgrims of peace."[3]

However, the *Catechism* reminds us that "agnosticism can sometimes include a certain search for God, but it can equally express indifferentism, a flight from the ultimate question of existence, and a sluggish moral conscience. Agnosticism is all too often equivalent to practical atheism" (CCC 2128). Both the agnostic and the weak atheist share the same position: lack of belief in God because there seem to be no good reasons to think God exists. Many agnostics identify as atheists, however, because a vibrant subculture exists among those who call themselves atheists.

As an "atheist," a non-believer might join a local club for atheists, visit atheist websites, or even wear clothes adorned with the red letter "A," which has become a common symbol for atheism. But unlike in Hawthorne's *Scarlett Letter*, this "A" is worn with pride. It often encompasses not just a lack of belief in God, but the belief that atheists are more rational than religious people. In fact, the philosopher Daniel Dennett, one of the pioneering "new atheists," proposed that atheists should instead be known as "brights," which tacitly implies that religious believers like you or Bishop Barron are "dims."[4]

We will discuss the philosophical underpinnings of atheism shortly, but first we should turn to the main source of contention between believers and atheists: the existence of God.

✝

## ARE WE ALL ATHEISTS?

You may have noticed that in his first talk, Bishop Barron spent a significant amount of time talking about God before discussing atheism. This is important because Catholics and atheists often don't agree about what the word "God" means.

For example, some atheists say, "You and I are both atheists. You are an atheist when it comes to mythological Gods like Zeus or Thor. I just happen to believe in one fewer God than you do." But recall what Bishop Barron said about Anselm's definition of God. St. Anselm of Canterbury defined God in his work *Monologion* as "that than which no greater can be thought."[5]

If God is defined in this way, then not only do Catholics not believe in deities like Zeus or Thor, we know these beings are not "God." They might be referred to as "gods," or beings that are merely the object of worship, but beings like Zeus and Thor are not *God*. God is "that than which no greater can be thought," and the gods of mythology could be greater if they had more to rule over, or if they were not constrained by time or space. Elevating beings like Zeus to the status of God is the same error the Galatians made when they, at one time, worshiped "things which by nature are not gods" (Gal 4:8).

The gods of mythology are just super-powered versions of human beings. In fact, the ancient Greek philosophers Plato and Aristotle reached this conclusion 2,400 years ago, when belief in these gods was still popular. The one true God, in contrast, is so unlike anything we know that when we try to think about him we, as Bishop Barron says, often get it wrong.

J.B. Phillips wrote a great little book in 1952 called *Your God Is Too Small*, which is a good way to describe how many people both past and present think of God. For example, St. Paul exhorted the Greeks in Athens to abandon their idols because, as he said, "The God who made the world and everything in it, being Lord of heaven and earth, does not live in shrines made by man, nor is he served by human hands, as though he needed anything, since he himself gives to all men life and breath and everything" (Acts 17:24-25).

Modern people may think they aren't like silly pagans who tried to trap God in tiny little boxes, but modern man commits his own errors that make God too small. Even if he conceives of God as having unlimited power, he still might think of him as an invisible genie that exists beyond the edge of the physical universe. To them, God is a kind of super-being that peers into our cosmos and uses his super-vision to see what his human pets are doing. But large as this God is, he is still too small.

He is not the God of classical theologians like St. Augustine or St. Thomas Aquinas, but is instead what sociologists Christian Smith and Melinda Denton call the god of "moralistic therapeutic deism." This god is simply a powerful being that created the world (deism), wants us to be good (moralistic), and exists to help us when we're in need (therapeutic). He's not *ipsum esse* ("the sheer act of being itself") who sustains all of existence through his perfect love. He's just a really powerful person.

While only about 2-5% of people identify as being atheists, many more people (about 20%) just say they are not religious. If they believe in God, it is probably the god of moralistic therapeutic deism. Sadly, even many religious people, including Catholics, think of God as this distant, deistic landlord whose job it is simply to keep the lights on and punish his tenants when they misbehave.

So what do we as Catholics really mean when we say, at every Sunday Mass, "I believe in one God"?

# ✝
## WHAT IS GOD?

Here is where the rich intellectual history of the Catholic Church bears its abundant harvest. For 2,000 years theologians and philosophers have peered into what the Lutheran theologian Rudolf Otto called *the mysterium tremendum et fascinans*, or "the fearful and fascinating mystery" of God.[6] While their insights help us talk about God, even their careful reflections only scratch the tip of the proverbial iceberg. As we discuss who God is, we must be careful and deliberate with the language we use. The *Catechism* states:

> Since our knowledge of God is limited, our language about him is equally so. We can name God only by taking creatures as our starting point, and in accordance with our limited human ways of knowing and thinking.
>
> All creatures bear a certain resemblance to God, most especially man, created in the image and likeness of God. The manifold perfections of creatures—their truth, their goodness, their beauty—all reflect the infinite perfection of God (CCC 40-41).

The goodness we observe in creatures gives us clues about what God is like (such as man's rational nature telling us that God is pure intellect). But this kind of thinking runs the risk of reducing God to a kind of super-creature. The truth is that the most radical difference between God and his creatures is not a difference in power or wisdom. Instead, it's the fact that while all creatures are defined by "what they are," God is defined as "that which is."

According to St. Thomas Aquinas, there is a difference between a thing's essence (what it is) and a thing's existence (that it is). You and I have a human essence, or what could be called a *human nature*. We are ordered towards distinctly human ends, such as rational thought and moral awareness.

While different creatures are ordered towards different ends, and thus have different essences, what they all have in common is that none of them has to exist. There could be a world without fish, or birds, or stars, or even people. But God is different. God is the being whose *essence is existence*. God is not one being in the universe, or even a being who exists outside of the universe in a special realm. Instead, God just is "existence," or in the words of Pope St. John Paul II, "the great 'Existent.'"[7]

This fundamental truth about God goes back to the beginning of his revelation to mankind. In the book of Genesis, God is shown to be an uncreated being who, unlike the other pagan deities, did not create the world by copulating with another god or by fighting a monster. Instead, God simply spoke the world into existence.

The world only exists because God exists, and it's impossible for God not to exist because he is existence. He just *is*. Now, that doesn't mean God is *identical* to the physical universe. That is a belief known as pantheism. Instead, God is *distinct* from a universe that both doesn't have to exist and only still exists because God wills that to be the case. That's why an atheist's demand that God's existence be proven scientifically is a non-starter. God is not a being in the universe that can be discovered through scientific investigation. He is instead Being itself, which sustains the universe, and his existence is demonstrated through philosophical reflection.

†

## GOD MADE IN MAN'S IMAGE

While atheism has been around in one form or another since ancient times, its exaltation in modern Western thought came about through the ideas of three famous thinkers: Ludwig Feuerbach, Karl Marx, and Jean-Paul Sartre.

Ludwig Feuerbach was a 19th-century philosopher whose contribution to the debate over the existence of God remains with us in the following phrase, "God did not make man in his image; we made God in our image."[8] Feuerbach's theory was that God is the ideal we all strive to achieve, either directly or indirectly. We desire to have complete control, total knowledge, and an impeccable character, and we think we'll never reach those goals unless there is a being like God who can help us. But in his 1848 work *The Essence of Christianity*, Feuerbach wrote:

> The divine being is nothing else than the human being, or rather, the human nature purified, freed from the limits of the individual man, made objective—i.e., contemplated and revered as another, a distinct being. All the attributes of the divine nature are, therefore, attributes of the human nature.[9]

We pray that God will let us share in his attributes, but Feuerbach says that is not enough. Instead, man can only reach his true potential when he leaves behind the projection of God he has made and recognizes his own internal divine potential. Feuerbach continues:

> In religion man seeks contentment; religion is his highest good. But how could he find consolation and peace in God if God were an essentially different being? How can I share the peace of a being if I am not of the same nature with him? If his nature is different from mine, his peace is essentially different—it is no peace for me.[10]

Now, Feuerbach would be correct if man worshipped "a god" or *a* being that is completely alien to us in every way. But scripture is clear that we, as Christians, can "partake in the divine nature" (2 Pet 1:4). The reason we can do that is because God is not "an essentially different being"—he is *being* itself! What St. Paul said to the Athenians is just as relevant to us today: "They should seek God, in the hope that they might feel after him and find him. Yet he is not far from each one of us, for 'In him we live and move and have our being'" (Acts 17:27).

In fact, Feuerbach's argument can be turned on its head. If God does not really exist, except in concept, and only then because we want to believe in him, then by extension the concept of atheism cannot be true, because many people *don't* want God to exist. Christopher Hitchens once said if God existed, he would feel like he lived in a police state,[11] and the philosopher Thomas Nagel once said, "I want atheism to be true and am made uneasy by the fact that some of the most intelligent and well-informed people I know are religious believers."[12]

But rather than reduce a person's belief system to his psychological motivations, we should just examine the evidence and see where it leads. When we do that we find that the universal human longing for God is not an argument against God's existence: it's actually an argument for it. The *Catechism* says, "The desire for God is written in the human heart, because man is created by God and for God; and God never ceases to draw man to himself. Only in God will he find the truth and happiness he never stops searching for" (CCC 27).

The *Catechism* goes onto say that "this 'intimate and vital bond of man to God' can be forgotten, overlooked, or even explicitly rejected by man," due to things like evil, sin or scandal (CCC 29). But even if the explicit desire for God is absent, there still remains a deep yearning for perfect belonging and love that nothing in this world can truly satisfy.

But why do we have this desire? Where did it come from? People like Feuerbach say it came from inside ourselves, but in the 20th century, some Christian apologists proposed a novel argument

for the existence of God based on this innate desire. They called it *the argument from desire.* Catholic philosophers Peter Kreeft and Ronald Tacelli formally put it this way:

1.  Every natural, innate desire in us corresponds to some real object that can satisfy that desire.

2.  But there exists in us a desire which nothing in time, nothing on earth, no creature can satisfy.

3.  Therefore there must exist something more than time, earth, and creatures, which can satisfy this desire.

4.  This something is what people call "God" and "life with God forever."[13]

Premise two seems very probable because most people, no matter how much money they earn, how many friends they have, or how much pleasure they chase, feel that they are never perfectly satisfied. We always want more, almost as if we were made for something greater.

Therefore, the argument hinges on the truth of premise one, which can be derived from a statement of the ancient Greek philosopher Aristotle: "Nature makes nothing in vain."[14] The sentiment was well known in Aristotle's time, and he used it to demonstrate that man's innate desire for justice and harmony could be achieved through his ability to reason. Aristotle argues that we wouldn't have the ability to reason unless there was something useful about which to reason.

Now, some people will object that we often have desires that could never, even in principle, be satisfied. After all, haven't most of us desired to fly like a bird or swim underwater with the agility of a fish? Couldn't the desire for God be just as unrealistic?

But Kreeft and Tacelli's point is that one of our *natural*, or *innate*, desires is for perfect happiness. These aren't mere flights of fancy, like the desire to fly. They are instead the core desires of our very being. When they aren't met they manifest themselves as painful longings and deficiencies like hunger, thirst, and loneliness.

It would be bizarre to agonize over our inability to fly, but it is not bizarre to suffer over the absence of food or friends. That's because these are innate desires that can, at least in principle, be satisfied. Since it is not bizarre to lament over how ultimately unsatisfying the material things in this life are, then this deepest desire could, at least in principle, be satisfied.

But how could it be satisfied? Ultimately, only God, the source of all goodness and the creator who intended our very existence, could satisfy such a deep longing for meaning and happiness. As St. Augustine said, "Our hearts are restless, Lord, until they rest in you."[15]

✝

## ATHEISTIC EXISTENTIALISM

While Feuerbach tried to understand religion as a mere projection of our internal desires, his disciple Karl Marx wanted to understand why we engage in this projection at all. He argued that the reason man clings to God even though God does not exist is because man needs God in order to endure the agonies of life. Marx said that God, and the promise of eternal life with him, was merely "the opium of the people."[16] For him, religion was a painkiller that didn't treat any of life's problems but merely served to distract people from what actually matters. If man is to face the trials of this life, Marx believed, he must first recognize that there is no God that can help him. The *Catechism* refers to versions of atheism like Marx's as ones that "look for the liberation of man through economic and social liberation." These forms of atheism "hold that religion, of its very nature, thwarts such emancipation by raising man's hopes in a future life, thus both deceiving him and discouraging him from working for a better form of life on earth" (CCC 2124).

This leads us to the thought of Jean-Paul Sartre, whom Bishop Barron referred to as the founder of "modern atheistic existentialism." What is existentialism? The core tenet of existentialism is that "existence precedes essence." Remember that the Catholic view of God is that God's essence, or what he is, is identical to his existence, or that he is. For creatures like us, we see that there is a difference between our existence and our essence. I am a human being, so I have a human essence. If I were to cease to exist, the essence of my humanity would not cease to exist with me. The essence of what I am, or my humanity, *precedes* my existence. It was here before I was born, and it will exist after I perish.

Existentialism completely flips this view around. My essence, or what I am, doesn't exist before I do as an idea for me to discover and follow. Instead, I alone determine who I am and what the purpose of my life is. Sartre was so committed to the view that humans must be

"free" to radically define their existence that he essentially said: If God exists, then I can't be free. But I am free, therefore God does not exist.

As Bishop Barron observes, this is a valid argument—which means it contains solid logic—but it is not a sound one, since the premises are false. It's simply not true that if God exists, then we can't be free. The *Catechism* teaches that "Atheism is often based on a false conception of human autonomy, exaggerated to the point of refusing any dependence on God. Yet, 'to acknowledge God is in no way to oppose the dignity of man, since such dignity is grounded and brought to perfection in God. . . .' 'For the Church knows full well that her message is in harmony with the most secret desires of the human heart'" (CCC 2126).

In fact, only if God exists can we be truly free. The *Catechism* says that freedom is "the power, rooted in reason and will, to act or not to act, to do this or that, and so to perform deliberate actions on one's own responsibility" (CCC 1731). Animals can choose to act according to instinct, but only man chooses to act responsibly and so uses his freedom to choose what is or is not good. As St. Paul says, "For you were called to freedom, brethren; only do not use your freedom as an opportunity for the flesh, but through love be servants of one another" (Gal 5:13).

But how can there be an "objective" good that we are free to choose if God does not exist? Sartre himself saw that this was a problem, and once said that:

> It must be considered obligatory *a priori* to be honest, not to lie, not to beat one's wife, to bring up children and so forth . . . . The existentialist, on the contrary, finds it extremely embarrassing that God does not exist, for there disappears with Him all possibility of finding values in an intelligible heaven. There can no longer be any good *a priori*, since there is no infinite and perfect consciousness to think it. It is nowhere written that "the good" exists, that one must be honest or must not lie, since we are now upon the plane where there are only men. Dostoevsky once wrote: "If God did not exist, everything would be permitted"; and that, for existentialism, is the starting point.[17]

Just as Feuerbach's argument from atheism could be converted into an argument for God, so can Sartre's. While Sartre was wrong about freedom being impossible without God, he was right that without God abstract concepts like "the good" or "objective morality" lose their metaphysical foundations.

Rather than embrace a bleak atheistic view of the world that says these things are just "useful fictions," we can instead make the following argument: if God does not exist, then there are no objective moral values—things like "the good" and "the right" do not exist; they are just fictional terms we apply to our feelings. But objective moral values do exist. There really is a way we ought to live, and there really is an objective difference between good and evil. Since these objective realties exist, it follows that an ultimate foundation for them, goodness and being itself, exists. Therefore, God exists.

This is just one of many arguments that can be made in defense of the claim that God exists. In the next lesson, we'll examine a powerful argument for the existence of God whose premises are derived from the most basic features of the universe itself.

## QUESTIONS FOR UNDERSTANDING

1. What is atheism? What is the difference between strong atheism, weak atheism, and agnosticism? (CCC 2123-2128)

2. What is the biggest difference between God and anything else in creation? How do atheists misunderstand God when they describe him as a being that has not been proven to exist?

3. How would you respond to this argument? "God is just something human beings invented so that they could feel better about themselves." How does the innate desire to believe in God serve as evidence for the existence of God? (CCC 27-29)

4. What does it mean to be free? How does God help us to be truly free? (CCC 1730-1734)

# QUESTIONS FOR APPLICATION

1. Is my view of God too small? Do I think of God as just "another creature" or as "the great Existent" who is deserving of *all* my love and worship?

2. Do I see God as someone who inhibits my freedom? If so, what in life have I put before God that I choose to serve instead of him?

3. How can I better communicate the reality of God to friends and family who identify as atheists or simply don't think God is very important in their lives?

# THE MYSTERY
## OF GOD

WORD
on FIRE

# THE PATHS TO GOD
## LESSON TWO OUTLINE

I.   INTRODUCTION
    A.  Second Vatican Council on God's Existence
    B.  Using Reason to Find God

II.  THE WAYS OF ST. THOMAS
    A.  Five Ways and the *Summa Theologiae*
    B.  Richard Dawkins's Critique

III. UNDERSTANDING CONTINGENCY
    A.  Definition
    B.  Necessity vs. Contingency
    C.  The Only Necessary Being
    D.  Argument for God's Existence

IV.  THE PRINCIPLE OF SUFFICIENT REASON
    A.  Examples
    B.  Richard Taylor's "Small Glowing Orb"
    C.  Why Does It Exsist?
    D.  Atheist Critique

V.   A QUESTION OF NECESSITY
    A.  Is the Universe Necessary or Contingent?
    B.  Fallacy of Composition
    C.  Quarks

VI.  BIG BANG EVIDENCE
    A.  Fr. George Lemaitre
    B.  Defining "Nothing"

## LESSON TWO
# *THE PATHS TO GOD*

The first Vatican Council dogmatically declared that God's existence can be known by reason alone. The *Catechism* teaches that,

> Created in God's image and called to know and love him, the person who seeks God discovers certain ways of coming to know him. These are also called proofs for the existence of God, not in the sense of proofs in the natural sciences, but rather in the sense of "converging and convincing arguments," which allow us to attain certainty about the truth (CCC 31).

The Catechism goes on to explain that while a specific individual might have difficulty knowing God exists (think of a child born in the atheistic Soviet Union), this does not mean that people in general cannot know God exists. Indeed, St. Paul wrote in his letter to the Romans that "Ever since the creation of the world, his invisible nature, namely, his eternal power and deity, has been clearly perceived in the things that have been made." (Rom 1:20).

But while God's existence can be known by reason, we must, as Bishop Barron says, not "over-rationalize" the case for his existence. We shouldn't make the mystery of God something that can be totally confined within the premises of a logical argument, even if such arguments can help us see that God exists. That is why it is more helpful to think of the arguments for the existence of God as "ways" or "paths" that lead seekers to a knowledge of God.

## THE WAYS OF ST. THOMAS

According to the *Catechism*, "These 'ways' of approaching God from creation have a twofold point of departure: the physical world, and the human person . . . . Starting from movement, becoming, contingency, and the world's order and beauty, one can come to a knowledge of God as the origin and the end of the universe" (CCC 31-32).

The Catholic Church does not endorse an official set of arguments for the existence of God, but the five arguments made by St. Thomas Aquinas in his *Summa Theologica* hold a special place in her history. While these "five ways," as they've been called, are perhaps the most famous part of the *Summa*, they are very brief. They comprise less than two pages of a work that is 3,500 pages long. Their brevity may explain why many introductory philosophy texts quote them in reference to the question of God's existence.

However, this is unfortunate because, as Thomistic scholar Edward Feser says, "Aquinas never intended [the five ways] to stand alone, and would probably have reacted with horror if told that future generations of students would be studying them in isolation, removed from their original immediate context in the *Summa Theologica* and the larger context of his work as a whole."[18] When atheists confront the five ways in an abbreviated and isolated form, they often think that they are easy to refute. For example, Richard Dawkins writes, "The five 'proofs' asserted by Thomas Aquinas in the thirteenth century don't prove anything, and are easily—though I hesitate to say so, given his eminence—exposed as vacuous."[19]

The problem with Dawkins's assertion is that the *Summa Theologica* was never meant to be a robust defense against non-Catholic objections (that was the subject of Aquinas's previous work the *Summa Contra Gentiles*). Instead, Aquinas tells us that the *Summa Theologica* was intended to be a short guide to theology for beginners. He writes, "Because the doctor of Catholic truth ought not only to teach the proficient, but also to instruct beginners . . . . we purpose in this book to treat of whatever belongs to the Christian religion, in such a way as may tend to the instruction of beginners."[20]

This means that atheists like Dawkins and others who criticize Thomas's arguments are usually attacking a "straw man." They think Aquinas's argument against atheism is too simple, when in reality Aquinas was just providing a helpful summary for novices, not a full-fledged rebuttal to critics. In this lesson we will discuss Bishop Barron's synthesis of Thomas's first three ways of coming to know that God exists, and answer the most common atheist objections.

# UNDERSTANDING CONTINGENCY

As opposed to St. Thomas's fourth way, which argues from creaturely perfections to the existence of God, and his fifth way, which argues from the orderliness of the natural world to a transcendent designer, the first three ways are *cosmological* arguments for the existence of God. They show that the existence of the universe itself (i.e., the "cosmos") gives us good reason to believe that God exists. Specifically, they show us that because the universe's existence is *contingent*, it follows that God exists.

What does it mean to be contingent? Simply put, a being is contingent if it depends on something else in order to exist. For example, you might hear someone say his Christmas vacation this year is contingent upon getting that Christmas bonus. If the boss doesn't give out the Christmas bonus, then the Christmas vacation will not happen. The Christmas vacation is contingent because it depends on the Christmas bonus in order to exist. If the Christmas bonus fails to exist, so does the Christmas vacation.

In fact, everything in this world is contingent, depending on something else in order to exist. You and I would not exist without water or air, but those things would not exist without the molecules that make up their chemical structure. Even the molecules that make up air or water depend on other fundamental forces in order to exist (like gravity or the strong nuclear force). Finally, those fundamental forces could have been different (i.e., they could have been more or less powerful), so even they depend on some other reality in order to explain why they exist.

Now that we understand what it means to be contingent, we can investigate the opposite of contingency, or *necessity*. Something is necessary if it depends on nothing else in order to exist. Because it depends on nothing in order to exist, a necessary being *must* exist. For example, the truth that 2+2=4 is a necessary truth. While it could be represented by different numerals (e.g. ii+ii=iv), the truth underlying the numerals is always the same. Other kinds of necessary truths are laws of logic, such as the law of non-contradiction, which says that, "No statement can be true and false at the same time in the same circumstance." These laws would always be true no matter what kind of world existed, which means they are necessary, not contingent.

Now, while there may be *truths* that are necessary, Christians have long argued that the only necessary *being* is God, because God is being itself. In fact, all necessary truths, including logical and mathematical truths, only exist because they come from the necessary, perfect, and unchanging mind of God.

Now that we are familiar with the concepts of contingency and necessity, we can examine the following argument for the existence of God:

**Step #1 – The universe demands an explanation for its existence.**

1. A contingent reality requires an explanation for why it exists.

2. The universe is a contingent reality.

3. Therefore, the universe requires an explanation for why it exists.

**Step #2 – God is the only possible explanation for the universe's existence.**

4. The explanation for the universe's existence cannot be an infinite number of other contingent realties.

5. Therefore, the explanation must be a necessary reality.

6. The only necessary reality that can explain the existence of all contingent realities is God.

**Conclusion**

7. Therefore, God exists.

Let's take a closer look at each of the premises, or statements that make up the argument from contingency.

†

# THE PRINCIPLE OF SUFFICIENT REASON

Premise one states, "A contingent reality requires an explanation for why it exists." When we observe objects or phenomena within the universe, we seek an explanation for why that object or phenomenon exists. When we see the magical brilliance of the Northern Lights, or even just the mundane newspaper on our doorstep, we naturally ask, "What caused this thing? Why does it exist?" We then seek an explanation in other familiar things in order to answer those questions.

Some explanations are readily apparent, such as the newspaper delivery boy who deposits the newspaper. Others might require research, like the photoelectric quality of particles in higher latitudes that causes the northern lights. Even if we don't know what the explanation is at first, we don't simply throw up our hands and say, "There is no explanation. That's just the way it is!" As Sherlock Holmes once said, "When you eliminate the impossible, whatever remains, however improbable, must be the truth."[21] The principle behind this maxim, which philosophers call the Principle of Sufficient Reason, is what drives modern science. Even if the scientist's ninety-ninth hypothesis fails to explain the data he observes, he knows there must be *some* explanation. He just hasn't found it yet.

But what's true of the explanations for little things is also true of the explanations for bigger things. The philosopher Richard Taylor asks us to imagine what we would do if we were walking through the woods and found a small glowing orb.[22] Like for the newspaper or the northern lights, we would ask, "Why does this thing exist?" We wouldn't just accept the answer, "Well, there is no reason. This little thing has just always existed." Okay, but why has *this particular thing* always existed? Why has it *always* existed?

We would be justified in asking these questions even if the orb were very large, say the size of a blimp, or even the size of an entire planet. Now, what if the orb were the size of the entire universe? We'd still ask the same question: "Why does it exist?" This shows that an atheist can't avoid the contingency argument for God by saying the universe "just exists," so we don't have to explain why it exists. That's not an explanation; it's instead an evasion of a valid question.

At this point an atheist might say that the universe is contingent and it does need an explanation for its existence, but the explanation isn't God. Instead, the whole universe could still be explained by just explaining why each contingent part exists. Atheist Paul Edwards once gave the example of five Eskimos visiting New York City in order to illustrate this point.[23] He says that if we can explain why each Eskimo is visiting the city then it's no mystery to explain why the whole group is visiting. For example, maybe one is there on business while another is there as a tourist. In regards to the universe, scientists may one day be able to explain why each part of the universe exists and as a result, they'll explain why the entire universe exists.

However, explaining why each part of the universe exists by referencing another part of the universe is like explaining the Eskimo's visits in this way, "Number five is following number four, who followed number three, who followed number two, who followed number one, who followed number five." Each member is explained but we still don't know why the *whole group* exists, just as explaining the universe through each of its parts doesn't explain why the *whole universe* exists in the first place.

# A QUESTION OF NECESSITY

We've come to the conclusion that contingent things require an explanation for why they exist. If the whole universe is contingent, then it needs an explanation for why it exists as well. But what if the universe was not contingent? An atheist could answer this argument by saying, "The universe is necessary. It simply has to exist. Therefore, there is no need to explain why the universe exists. That's just the way it is." This is where premise two comes into the discussion. It says, "The universe is a contingent reality." The problem with the atheist's reply is that there is no good reason to think the universe is necessary. There are also good reasons to think the universe is contingent, or that it depends on something else in order to exist.

One reason to believe the universe is contingent is that everything that exists in the universe is contingent. From planets and stars to people and plants, none of these things had to exist and we can imagine a universe not containing them. If the universe could have been a barren wasteland, then isn't it possible that there simply could have been no universe at all? An atheist could object that this kind of reasoning commits what philosophers call the "fallacy of composition." He might say, "Just because everything in the universe is contingent doesn't mean that the entire universe is contingent. After all, just because every man in a country has a mother, it doesn't follow that the country itself has a mother. The property of a thing's parts doesn't always apply to the whole."

Now, it's true that what is true of a thing's parts is not *always* true of the whole, but sometimes it is. For example, if every brick in a wall is red, then the whole wall will be red. Likewise, it seems intuitive that if every object in the universe is contingent, then the entire universe is contingent, or the whole universe depends on something else in order to exist.

An atheist might also claim that the contingent nature of all the objects in the universe only proves that those objects themselves didn't have to exist. Perhaps the tiny particles that make up all the objects in the universe had to exist even if they never formed any particular object.

But why should we believe that? Couldn't those tiny particles have been different? The smallest particles we are aware of are called quarks (they're even smaller than atoms and electrons). Scientists believe there are six different kinds of quarks and give them colorful names like the "up quark" the "charm quark" and the "strange quark" (as if they all aren't strange to begin with). Couldn't there have been just four quarks? Couldn't there have been a seventh one? Some theoretical physicists believe that the universe is, or at least could have been, ultimately composed of tiny sub-atomic strings and not quarks. The fact that we can sensibly imagine the universe, including its fundamental particles, being different is evidence of the universe's contingent nature.

For example, think of a triangle and its three sides. The sides might be equal or they could be of differing lengths, but you can't think of a triangle without it having three sides. You can think of a shape with more or less sides, but it wouldn't be a triangle. This means that the three sides of a triangle are necessary. While it would be normal to ask why a particular triangle is blue or why it was drawn so poorly, it would be odd to ask why a certain triangle has three sides. Having three sides is just what it means to be a triangle.

Now consider the question, "Why does the universe exist?" It's not an odd question like, "Why does that triangle have three sides?" It is instead a profound and meaningful question. The famous contemporary philosopher Derek Parfit writes, "Why is there a universe at all? It might have been true that nothing ever existed: no living beings, no stars, no atoms, not even space or time. When we think about this, it can seem astonishing that anything exists."[24]

The fact that this question can be asked shows that the universe is not necessary. If the universe had to exist, if that is the only way that reality could have been, then we wouldn't ask why the universe exists anymore than we would ask why triangles have three sides. But since we can ask that question, then we are justified in searching for an explanation for the universe beyond the space, time, matter, and energy that make up the universe.

✝

## BIG BANG EVIDENCE

One requirement for a being to be necessary is that it can't have come into existence. If it did then it would owe its existence to another being since nothing can bring itself into existence. It would depend on something else in order to exist, or it would be contingent, not necessary. But we have scientific evidence that the universe began to exist in an event called the Big Bang.

Originally developed by a Belgian priest named Fr. George Lemaitre, this theory (which Fr. Lemaitre called "the primeval atom") does not refer to an explosion of matter within space. Instead, it refers to an expansion of space, matter, energy, and even time itself from nothing at all. But if the universe came from nothing then it requires a cause, or as Thomas says, "If the world and motion have a first beginning, some cause must clearly be posited to account for this origin of the world and of motion."[25]

An atheist might say in response that the universe could have come "from nothing," without any cause, by invoking the science of quantum physics. He might say that very tiny particles have been observed popping into existence from nothing so our universe could have come to be in a similar manner. But by "nothing" the atheist really means a "quantum vacuum" which is actually a fluctuating low-level energy field, not "nothing." Philosopher and theoretical physicist David Albert writes:

> [V]acuum states—no less than giraffes or refrigerators or solar systems—are particular arrangements of *elementary physical stuff*. . . . [T]he fact that particles can pop in and out of existence, over time, as those [quantum] fields rearrange themselves, is not a whit more mysterious than the fact that fists can pop in and out of existence, over time, as my fingers rearrange themselves. And none of these poppings—if you look at them aright—amount to anything even remotely in the neighborhood of a creation from nothing."[26]

Even if the universe emerged from the Big Bang, it still requires an explanation for why it exists. And, as we'll see, positing an infinite series of causes before the Big Bang does nothing to solve the problem.

## PROBLEMS WITH INFINITY

Since we've shown that contingent things require an explanation for why they exist, and the universe itself is contingent because it didn't have to exist, then it follows that the universe requires some kind of explanation for why it exists.

One rejoinder to this argument would be that the Big Bang that spawned our universe came from a previously existing universe. But when pressed about the origin of *that* universe an atheist might say that it came from another universe just as we came from that universe. Of course, when pressed enough, an atheist would have to admit that his explanation inevitably becomes an endless string of causes stretching backwards infinitely through time, since we can always ask, "But where did *that* cause come from?"

It won't do to simply say there were an infinite number of causes for our universe. That's because just as an infinite number of zeroes does not equal the number one, an infinite number of incomplete explanations does not equal a complete explanation. This is why premise four of our argument says that, "The explanation for the universe's existence cannot be an infinite number of other contingent realties."

Here's an illustration to help explain why that's the case. Suppose you and a friend are walking along railroad track and you see a boxcar being pulled along the railroad tracks. Your friend might ask, "What's pulling that boxcar?" Suppose you were to reply, "Well, the boxcar in front of it." Your friend would naturally ask, "But what's pulling *that* boxcar?" You answer, "Um, the boxcar in front of *that* boxcar . . ." and so on and so on.

Hopefully you can see the futility of this "infinite regress" explanation. It simply "passes the buck" and never provides an adequate explanation for why all the boxcars are moving at all. But what does this have to do with the universe?

Each boxcar on the train is like a contingent universe. Just as a boxcar can't move itself, our universe can't explain its own existence. The universe must instead be explained by something else, just as the boxcar must be pulled by something else. But even if the boxcar were attached to an infinitely long train of boxcars, that would not explain anything, since now we would just have an infinite number of boxcars whose movement we have to explain! When it comes to universes, an infinite number of universes does nothing to ultimately answer the question "Why does anything exist at all?" Invoking such a regress doesn't make the problem easier for the atheist to explain—it makes it infinitely worse!

But what about God? Couldn't an atheist object that invoking him to explain why the universe exists results in the same problem? Couldn't he say, "Why does God exist? If God caused the universe, then what caused God?" Here we must remember one of the fundamental truths that Bishop Barron shared with us about God—God is not just one being among others. If he were, then this objection would have merit, since God's existence would also have to be

explained. But God just is "being" itself, so it makes sense that God must exist. God can't fail to exist because he is existence.

Just as the boxcars all move because there is something that pulls them which relies on nothing else for motion (i.e., a locomotive), our world exists because there is something that gives existence to all things but receives existence from nothing, for it just *is* existence. As Aquinas would say, "this everyone understands to be God."

†

# AN ARGUMENT FROM INTELLECT

Suppose an atheist were to grant that the universe has a cause for its existence that is not contingent, or just another universe, but is necessary. It has to be something that by its very nature has to exist and depends on nothing else in order to exist. But from this description how do we arrive at the conclusion that the necessary explanation of the universe is a personal God? How do we know that the necessary cause of the universe loves and cares about human beings?

While God's revelation through Christ, Scripture, and the Church can help us know this truth in general, another argument can help us know that God is a personal being. The *Catechism* teaches that the universe's contingency and order provides evidence for the existence of God, but it also teaches that "[W]ith his openness to truth and beauty, his sense of moral goodness, his freedom and the voice of his conscience, with his longings for the infinite and for happiness, man questions himself about God's existence. In all this he discerns signs of his spiritual soul. The soul, the 'seed of eternity we bear in ourselves, irreducible to the merely material', can have its origin only in God" (CCC 33).

As Bishop Barron noted, Bernard Lonergan's arguments for God start from the experience of human beings and demonstrate that we are ordered in our understanding and nature towards God himself. Similar to the argument from desire, Lonergan's argument states that human beings have an insatiable desire to know the world in which we live. It's not enough for us to simply know how things work. We want to know the deeper foundations of reality. As Bishop Barron explained, we might ask what a certain piece of technology is, but then we want to know what "technology" is. When we learn that it involves tools arranged to accomplish certain goods, we want to know about the deeper concepts of "tools" and especially "the good." Ultimately, we understand that these realities are kinds of beings, and so we want to know what "being" itself is. That leads us to know that being is not inanimate matter or a blind personal force, but pure, unrestricted understanding and existence itself. God is the dynamic reality that motivates us to intelligently comprehend all that he has created.

At the end of the day, however, it's important to remember that the arguments for the existence of God only take us so far. James 2:19 says, "You believe that God is one; you do well. Even the demons believe—and shudder." There is a difference between believing God exists and believing *in* God. The *Catechism* concludes,

> Man's faculties make him capable of coming to a knowledge of the existence of a personal God. But for man to be able to enter into real intimacy with him, God willed both to reveal himself to man and to give him the grace of being able to welcome this revelation in faith. The proofs of God's existence, however, can predispose one to faith and help one to see that faith is not opposed to reason (CCC 35).

## QUESTIONS FOR UNDERSTANDING

1. What does the Church teach about knowing the existence of God from reason alone? How do atheists sometimes misunderstand the arguments made by St. Thomas Aquinas for the existence of God? (CCC 31-35)

2. What is the difference between contingency and necessity? Why is God necessary while the universe is contingent?

3. Why does the universe require an explanation beyond itself in order to explain why it exists?

4. Why can't the explanation for the universe just be an infinite number of other universes or causes?

5. How does the insatiable human desire to know the world point back to the existence of a personal God?

# QUESTIONS FOR APPLICATION

1.  What are the biggest obstacles that prevent atheists and non-believers from coming to know that God exists? Are they intellectual, spiritual, moral, emotional, or a combination of these factors?

2.  What is the difference between having faith that God exists and having faith in God? Which does your faith most closely resemble?

3.  Are you willing to share the "ways" to God with non-believing friends and family members? If not, what is holding you back?

# THE MYSTERY
## OF GOD

WORD
*on* FIRE

# THE DIVINE ATTRIBUTES
## LESSON THREE OUTLINE

I.  INTRODUCTION
    A. *Catechism* on Speaking About God

II. GOD IS NECESSARY
    A. "Life In Himself"
    B. Moses and the Burning Bush
    C. I Am Who I Am
    D. Being Itself (*Ipsum Esse*)

III. GOD IS SIMPLE
    A. Richard Dawkins and Complexity
    B. Infinite Simplicity
    C. Does God Have Parts?
    D. St. Anselm's Answer

IV. GOD IS INFINITE
    A. Inexhaustible and Inscrutable
    B. Infinite God vs. Mathematical Infinity
    C. Why Only One God?

V.  GOD IS SPIRIT
    A. Immaterial
    B. God is Everywhere
    C. Lord and Creator of All Things

VI. GOD IS ETERNAL
    A. What is Time?
    B. Everlasting God
    C. God Before Time?
    D. Unchanging and Timeless God

VII. GOD IS ALL-KNOWING
   A. Omniscience
   B. Joseph and God's Knowledge of the Future
   C. Freedom vs. Omniscience
   D. Calvinist Protestant Answer
   E. Open Theists's Answer
   F. Boeuthius's Answer

VIII. GOD IS ALL-POWERFUL
   A. Catechism and Omnipotence
   B. Can God Do Anything We Imagine?
   C. Only the Logically Possible
   D. Fatherly Omnipotence

LESSON THREE

# THE DIVINE ATTRIBUTES

Since God's existence can be known through reason, the Church can express "her confidence in the possibility of speaking about him to all men and with all men" (CCC 39). However, the *Catechism* also cautions us to remember that

> God transcends all creatures. We must therefore continually purify our language of everything in it that is limited, image-bound or imperfect, if we are not to confuse our image of God—"the inexpressible, the incomprehensible, the invisible, the ungraspable"—with our human representations. Our human words always fall short of the mystery of God (CCC 42).

In this lesson we will heed that advice by exploring God's different attributes, the unique qualities that distinguish God and describe who he is.

## GOD IS NECESSARY

As we learned in the previous lesson, something is necessary if it depends on nothing else for its own existence. We know that our contingent, dependent world requires a necessary being like God in order to exist, but scripture also teaches us about God's necessity. St. Paul refers to God as "the King of kings and Lord of lords, who alone has immortality and dwells in unapproachable light" (1 Tim 6:15-16). Jesus said, "For as the Father has life in himself, so he has granted the Son also to have life in himself" (John 5:26). Who else but a necessary being could have "life in himself" and alone possess immortality?

Perhaps the most beautiful display of God's necessary existence is seen in his exchange with Moses in the third chapter of the book of Exodus. After having fled from Egypt many years

earlier, Moses was living as a shepherd in Midian when one day he caught sight of a bush that was on fire but not consumed. When Moses approached the bush, God spoke to him and told Moses to return to Egypt and free his people from their bondage.

From Moses' perspective, God wanted him to go and defy the god of the Egyptians, or the Pharaoh. Moses knew that his fellow Hebrews would want to know which deity was going to free them among the pantheon of gods worshipped at that time. So Moses asked for God's name, hoping it would reveal God's power and ability to overcome the Egyptians. God's surprising answer showed that he is radically different than any other creature, idol, or god. He said to Moses, "I AM WHO AM. . . . Say this to the people of Israel, 'I AM has sent me to you'" (Ex 3:14).

According to the *Catechism*, God's revelation as "I AM WHO AM" affirms his unique identity:

> The Greek Septuagint translation of the Hebrew Scriptures, and following it the Church's Tradition, understood the divine name in this sense: God is the fullness of Being and of every perfection, without origin and without end. All creatures receive all that they are and have from him; but he alone is his very being, and he is of himself everything that he is (CCC 213).

God's necessary existence as *being itself* (what Thomas calls *ipsum esse*) tells us something else about what God is like. While created beings are defined by the kind of parts they have and cease to be when their parts are disassembled, God has no parts. God cannot cease to exist precisely because he just *is* being and cannot be reduced to any simpler component parts. Theologians refer to this attribute as God's *simplicity*.

## GOD IS SIMPLE

*The God Delusion*, Richard Dawkins's popular atheist book, makes an argument against God in which Dawkins describes him as "the ultimate Boeing 747."[27] The name comes from an argument sometimes proffered by believers who say that just as a 747 jet airplane is too complex to have been created by chance alone (such as by a tornado sweeping through a junkyard), our much more complex universe could not have originated by chance alone either, and so it must have God as a designer. Dawkins thinks, however, that this line of reasoning can be used to *disprove* God's existence. He writes,

> A designer God cannot be used to explain organized complexity because any God capable of designing anything would have to be complex enough to demand the same kind of explanation in his own right. God presents an infinite regress from which he cannot help us to escape.[28]

This argument fails because God is not a complex object that requires an explanation outside of himself. In 1215 the Fourth Lateran Council declared,

> We firmly believe and simply confess that there is only one true God, eternal and immeasurable, almighty, unchangeable, incomprehensible and ineffable, Father, Son, and Holy Spirit, three persons but *one absolutely simple essence, substance, or nature* [emphasis added].[29]

God just is being itself and so his existence and nature are united in one simple essence, or state of being, which explains its own existence.[30] Remember, as Bishop Barron explained, creatures all differ in their essences, or what they are, but they all are similar in that none of them has to exist. God's essence, or what he is, however, is simply *that he is*, or that he must exist. God exists because that is what he is, or to say it another way, God just *is* existence itself in all its infinite simplicity.

Now, to Dawkins's credit, he is aware of this response, but thinks it can be defeated. He writes,

> A God capable of continuously monitoring and controlling the individual status of every particle in the universe *cannot* be simple. His existence is going to need a mammoth explanation in its own right. Worse (from the point of view of simplicity), other corners of God's giant consciousness are simultaneously preoccupied with the doings and emotions and prayers of every single human being—and whatever intelligent aliens there might be on other planets in this and 100 billion other galaxies.[31]

Dawkins also quotes Christian philosophers like Richard Swinburne who agree with him on the point that if God exists, then he cannot be simple.

What's ironic is that while Dawkins and Swinburne disagree about whether God exists, they are united in holding a mistaken view of God's nature. They believe God is just an infinitely powerful person. In fact, in Richard Swinburne's book *The Coherence of Theism* he thinks that, with a good enough imagination, we can imagine what it's like to be God! This journey to virtual godhood begins by slowly imagining what it's like to not feel any pain or loss. Then, imagine what it's like to acquire new abilities (like being able to know everyone's thoughts). Swinburne concludes this thought experiment by saying, "Surely anyone can thus conceive of himself becoming an omnipresent spirit."[32]

Now, if God was just a person like you or me, albeit an infinite, omnipresent spirit-person, then an atheist like Richard Dawkins would be justified in wondering how such a person could be "simple." After all, if people like us are complex given what our minds can do, then how much more complex would God be given what he can do! But God is not a super-being who has an invisible "consciousness" that keeps track of his thoughts and actions. He isn't *a* being with distinct parts at all, because if God had parts he could change or be reduced to something more basic than those parts.

Instead, as St. Anselm of Canterbury declares,

> [T]here are no parts in you, Lord: neither are You many, but You are so much one and the same with Yourself that in nothing are You dissimilar with Yourself. Indeed, You are unity itself not divisible by any mind. Life and wisdom and the other [attributes], then, are not parts of You, but all are one and each of them is wholly what You are and what all the others are.[33]

Anselm's claim is that God is not divided in any way, not even by his attributes. This means God's power is identical to his goodness, which is identical to his knowledge, which is identical to his existence, which is identical to all of God's other attributes. God is perfect unity without division. He is *ipsum esse*: the great I AM, or simply being itself.

Of course, as humans we speak of God as if he had different parts (like his will or his knowledge as being distinct parts of him) because our own minds are limited. We have to speak this way out of convenience in order to sensibly talk about God. The *Catechism* says, "Our language is using human modes of expression; nevertheless it really does attain to God himself, though unable to express him in his infinite simplicity" (CCC 43).

So, Dawkins's "ultimate 747" argument against God doesn't just crash, it can't even get off the ground because it is aimed at an incorrect concept of God—something even other atheists recognize. The philosopher Erik Wielenberg writes, "The central weakness of Dawkins's Gambit, then, is that it is aimed primarily at proving the nonexistence of a being that is unlike the God of traditional monotheism in some important ways. . . . In light of this, I must side with those critics of *The God Delusion* who have judged Dawkins's Gambit to be a failure."[34]

✝

## GOD IS INFINITE

Since God is undivided being itself, it follows that God exists without limits, that he is infinite. What does this mean? To be *finite* is to have a measurable or conceivable limit. The number of grains of sand on the earth is a huge number, but it has a limit (it can't be larger than the number of atoms on the earth, for example). Therefore, the number of grains of sand on the earth is finite. So, if the finite is defined as that which has limits, then the "in-finite," or infinity, is that which has no limit. For example, it's not possible to even imagine someone counting and reaching "the last number." There is no such number because the number of numbers is without limit; it is infinite.

When it comes to God, everything we know about him—his power, wisdom, knowledge, love, and goodness—is infinite. There is no limit to how much we can know about God (he is inexhaustible) and no way for us to anticipate God's limitless plans for us (he is inscrutable). Finally, there is no limit to the wonder and amazement we have in thinking about God as perfect being itself (he is awe-inspiring).

It's important to remember that God's infinite nature is different than the mathematical concept of infinity. While numbers are infinite because there is no limit to how many of them there are, God is not an infinite collection of anything (that would negate his simplicity). God is not, for example, infinite because he has an unlimited amount of facts in his mind or because he has an unlimited amount of "power-units" at his disposal. Instead, God is infinite because he is not limited in any aspect of his being. Nothing limits God's power, his knowledge, or any other aspect of his existence.

From the fact that God is not limited in any way, it also follows that there can only be one God. If another God existed, then these two beings would limit one another in some way, and so neither could be infinite. Even if they were equally powerful, the ability to distinguish between these two beings would show that each lacked something the other had. Recognizing what each being lacked would also be the only way we could conceptually distinguish between them. Since God is not a being that competes with other beings but is instead infinite being itself, it follows that there is only one God.

✝

## GOD IS SPIRIT

One of the limits we possess as human beings is spatial in nature. For example, we might hear a frustrated parent say, "I'm sorry, but I can't be in two places at once!" While humans are limited in where they can be due to their physical bodies, God is not limited in this way. Instead, God is immaterial; he exists without a physical body. That does not mean that God is a vapor who exists without a body in a certain location, like Casper the Friendly Ghost. It just means that God does not exist solely in one particular place. In Jeremiah 23:24 God asks, "Can a man hide himself in secret places so that I cannot see him? Do I not fill heaven and earth?" Jesus himself taught us that, "God is spirit" (John 4:24), and told his disciples that "a spirit has not flesh and bones" (Luke 24:39).

To say that God is everywhere does not mean that he is equivalent to everything. That's pantheism, which the Pontifical Council on Interreligious Dialogue defined as the belief that "every element of the universe is divine, and the divinity is equally present in everything. There is no space in this view for God as a distinct being in the sense of classical theism."[35]

One reason to reject pantheism is that God created the universe, and nothing can create itself. In 2 Maccabees 7:28, we read, "Look at the heavens and the earth and see everything that is in them, and recognize that God did not make them out of things that existed." In Colossians 1:16 we learn that "In him all things were created, in heaven and on earth, visible and invisible." An early Christian text called *The Shepherd of Hermas*, written around the year

80 A.D., says, "Believe first of all that God is one, that he created all things and set them in order and brought out of nonexistence into existence everything that is, and that he contains all things while he himself is uncontained."[36]

The 2nd-century Church father Theophilus of Antioch said, "What great thing were it, if God made the world out of existing matter? Even a human artist, when he obtains material from someone, makes of it whatever he pleases. But the power of God is made evident in this, that he makes whatever he pleases out of what does not exist, and the giving of life and movement belongs to none other but to God alone."[37]

If God were a limited, physical being, then he could not create all things, because he would depend on space and time in order to exist as an embodied entity. These realties would have to exist independently of God and be created by either another being, or be as eternal as God but not exist under his control. However, since God is spirit and is not made of matter, he can be Lord over all things and create all things, including space and time.[38] The *Catechism* affirms that, "God needs no pre-existent thing or any help in order to create, nor is creation any sort of necessary emanation from the divine substance. God creates freely 'out of nothing'" (CCC 296).

✝

## GOD IS ETERNAL

One simple definition of time is "that which measures change." The most common object we associate with time is a clock, whose minute and hour hands constantly change. As these hands slowly tick forward we watch the future that we imagine briefly become the present that we experience until it becomes the past that we remember. Through this unstoppable "march of time" we observe both things and people changing, growing, moving, becoming, and ceasing to be. The 14th-century English novelist Geoffrey Chaucer said it best when he wrote, "Time and tide wait for no man."[39]

So how is God related to time? We've seen that because God created space he is not limited by it, and so he is immaterial. Similarly, since God created time this means he is not limited by that either, thereby making him eternal. Now, there are two ways to think about God being eternal. First, there is the idea of God being *everlasting*, which means God always has existed and will never go out of existence. The Bible describes this kind of eternal existence when it says, "from everlasting to everlasting you are God" (Ps 90:2) or "you are the same, and your

years have no end" (Ps 102:28). The four living creatures in the book of Revelation never cease to sing, "Holy, holy, holy, is the Lord God Almighty, who was and is and is to come!" (Rev 4:8).

But if God has an everlasting existence, then what was he doing before he created the world? Was he just sitting around for infinite ages waiting for the perfect moment to say "Let there be light"? St. Augustine jokingly answered this question: "He was fashioning Hell for people who ask questions like that."[40] Augustine then admits that he's heard this reply before and that it only serves to evade the force of the critic's question. He then tackles the question head on by arguing that God wasn't doing anything before he created the world. That's because there was no time before God created it, and change only takes place in time. Augustine writes, "If before heaven and earth there was no time, why is it asked, What didst Thou then? For there was no 'then' when time was not."[41]

Before God created physical beings like us, or even spiritual beings like angels, he existed as perfect love and being. Since God is the infinite and perfect act of being, he has no needs, no deficiencies, no limits, and no imperfections. This means God doesn't change, because change is something that imperfect and limited beings undergo in order to adapt to their circumstances. God himself said to the prophet Malachi, "I the Lord do not change" (Mal 3:6), and the letter to the Hebrews describes Jesus, the God-man, as being "the same yesterday and today and forever" (Heb 13:8).

Since time is a measure of change and God does not change, it follows that God is not subject to time in any way. A God who slowly marched through time like us would be limited—a prisoner of the time he created. Instead, Catholic theologians and philosophers have traditionally taught that God is eternal in the sense that he is *timeless*. This means that just as God does not exist in any particular spatial location, he does not exist in any particular temporal location either. God simply exists without change in a perfect, timeless moment. Even though God does not change, his grace and love that flow perfectly from him are still felt in our time-bound world, in every passing moment.[42]

# GOD IS ALL-KNOWING

Since God sustains everything that exists and is aware of every moment in the past, present, and future due to his timeless existence, then it naturally follows that God is all-knowing. This attribute, which is also called omniscience, means that God knows every real or possibly real thing. Psalm 147:5 says that God's "understanding is beyond measure," and the book of Hebrews tells us that "No creature is concealed from him, but everything is naked and exposed to the eyes of him to whom we must render an account" (Heb 4:13, NAB).

In Genesis 50:20 Joseph tells the brothers who sold him into slavery, "You meant evil against me; but God meant it for good, to bring it about that many people should be kept alive, as they are today." God could not have meant Joseph's enslavement to be for good unless he knew that this event would cause Joseph to become a leader in Egypt and save his people in the future. This shows that God's omniscience includes infallible knowledge of the future.

As Bishop Barron says, God's knowledge isn't derived from anything else. God doesn't observe the world in order to learn what's true about it. Instead, God's knowledge is immediate and comes from his immanent and loving presence, which sustains everything in existence.

Now, some people believe that if God knows the future, then we can't be free. They think that because God knows today what I will do tomorrow, then whatever happens tomorrow is "locked in," since God can never be wrong. My choice for tomorrow is already set today; I am not free to make a different choice tomorrow.

There are two unacceptable solutions to this puzzle. On the one hand, we could side with certain Protestant Christians, such as Calvinists, who say that God knows the future because he has determined everything we will ever do. However, this would negate the freedom God gave us (CCC 1730) and make God directly responsible for our sins, even though the Bible says God tempts no one to sin (Jas 1:13). On the other hand, we could side with the so-called "open theists" who say that God doesn't know the future but is prepared for anything that might happen (i.e., God is just an all-powerful Boy Scout). Between these views the *Catechism* teaches that, "To God, *all moments of time* are present in their immediacy. When therefore he establishes his eternal plan of 'predestination', he includes in it each person's *free response* to his grace" (CCC 600, emphasis added).

In the 6th century, the Catholic philosopher Boethius proposed a resolution to this problem that is best understood through a modern analogy. Imagine a man in a tower who watches an entire parade pass by on the street beneath him. While the people on the street can only observe one part of the parade at a time, the man in the tower can observe the whole thing at once. Likewise, just as you or I can only observe the present, God can see the past, present, and future all in one timeless moment.[43]

Boethius defines God's eternal life as "the simultaneously whole and perfect possession of interminable life."[44] Therefore, it's incorrect to say that God knows "today" what I will do tomorrow because God possesses all of his temporal life—past, present, and future—at once. God is outside of time, so he "sees" my actions in both the past, present, and future at the same "time," because all times are immediately present to God, who exists in a timeless and changeless state.

Another example may help. If you observed me buying a car in the present, your observation would not negate my freedom—I still would freely buy the car. Similarly, when God observes me in the future, choosing to do the same thing, he does not negate my freedom to act in that time either.

Now, it's important to remember that God does not casually observe us in a celestial tower as time ticks by, thinking about what he will do. Thinking is an activity that imperfect, temporal beings engage in as they try to understand the world around them. God, however, is pure understanding itself. God is the infinite, perfect act of being that nothing, not even time or space, can constrain or limit.

✝

## GOD IS ALL-POWERFUL

God upholds and sustains every single being that exists, from the proton to the president. As Colossians 1:17 says, "He is before all things, and in him all things hold together." Since God sustains all of existence, he is all-powerful, or able to bring about any possible state of affairs in the world he sustains. The *Catechism* tells us that,

Of all the divine attributes, only God's omnipotence is named in the Creed: to confess this power has great bearing on our lives. We believe that his might is *universal*, for God who created everything also rules everything and can do everything (CCC 268).

Other passages in scripture affirming God's omnipotence include the ending of the book of Job, where the Lord's humble and afflicted servant says, "I know that you can do all things, and that no purpose of yours can be thwarted" (Job 42:2). God's omnipotence is also evidenced at the Annunciation, where the angel Gabriel assures the Blessed Virgin Mary that "with God nothing will be impossible" (Luke 1:37). This was later echoed in Jesus' teaching about salvation and his promise that "all things are possible with God" (Mark 10:27).

Now, some people will ask, "If God can do anything, then could he destroy himself? Could he command us to do evil? Could he make a rock so big that not even he could lift it?" But saying that God's power is not limited is not the same as saying he can do anything we can imagine. That was the mistake of some medieval philosophers such as Al-Ghazali or William of Ockham, who thought that God's infinite nature meant that not even logic could limit him. They thought that to be truly omnipotent, God had to be able to do the logically impossible like destroy himself or declare evil actions to be good.

But God's will is not isolated from the rest of his attributes. In fact, because God is simple, his will (what he chooses to do) is the same as his intellect, which is the same as his goodness. They are all the same because they are the consequences of existing as pure being. If God were simply *a* being, he would be limited and lack certain goods or ideas in the intellect, but since God just *is being*, he lacks nothing, including intelligence or goodness. God doesn't just fully possess these things, but rather he *is* these things. As the *Catechism* says,

> God's almighty power is in no way arbitrary: "In God, power, essence, will, intellect, wisdom, and justice are all identical. Nothing therefore can be in God's power which could not be in his just will or his wise intellect" (CCC 271).

Therefore, God cannot will to do something that contradicts his perfect and good nature.

St. Augustine even said that God "cannot do some things for the very reason that he is omnipotent."[45] If God created rocks he couldn't lift or destroyed himself, then he would cease to be all-powerful and become limited in some way. Omnipotence, therefore, only refers to God having the power to make actual anything that is logically possible. This includes things that are impossible only for creatures (i.e., the naturally impossible, like raising the dead) but not

the logically impossible, like square-circles or married bachelors. Any definition of omnipotence that involves what simply can't exist under any circumstance (i.e., logical impossibilities) would contradict God's perfect nature and be an unsuitable definition of this attribute.

Finally, God doesn't wield his power like an insecure dictator we should fear. Instead, God's power is made known through his infinite love for us that is not hindered in any way but is ordered towards our good and the good of all creatures. As the *Catechism* says,

> God reveals his fatherly omnipotence by the way he takes care of our needs; by the filial adoption that he gives us. . . . Once our reason has grasped the idea of God's almighty power, it will easily and without any hesitation admit everything that [the Creed] will afterwards propose for us to believe (CCC 270, 274).

## QUESTIONS FOR UNDERSTANDING

1.  What do we mean when we say that God is necessary? How does the name that God revealed to Moses hint at his necessity? (Ex 3:14, John 1:3, Col 1:15-17, CCC 212-213)

2.  What does it mean when we say that God is infinite and simple?

3.  What does it mean when we say that God is immaterial and eternal? How would God be limited if he were not immaterial or eternal? (Jer 23:24, Ps 90:2, John 4:24, Heb 13:8, Rev 4:8, CCC 296, CCC 300-301, CCC 600)

4.  What do we mean when we say that God is all-powerful and all-knowing? Are there any limits to what God can do? Does God's knowledge limit man's freedom? (Gen 50:20, Luke 1:37, Col 1:17, Heb 4:13, CCC 269-271, CCC 600)

# QUESTIONS FOR APPLICATION

1.  Do I truly believe that God is infinite and all-powerful, or do I put limits on God and act as if there are some things he can't do or is not concerned about?

2.  Are there times when I doubt that God is all-loving? How can I better trust in God and in his promises?

3.  Write in your own words a description of God's attributes and an explanation of what each one means. Use this in preparation for discussion with those who question the existence of God.

# THE MYSTERY
## OF GOD

# PROVIDENCE AND THE PROBLEM OF EVIL

## LESSON FOUR OUTLINE

I. INTRODUCTION
   A. Challenge of Skeptics

II. THE NATURE OF PROVIDENCE
   A. Story of Katie Lentz and "Miracle Priest"
   B. Miracles
   C. Providence

III. THE PROBLEM OF PROVIDENCE
   A. Just Randomness or Luck?
   B. Occasionalists and Direct Causality
   C. St. Thomas Aquinas and Primary Causality
   D. Secondary Causes

IV. THE PROBLEM OF EVIL
   A. David Hume's Challenge
   B. Rabbi Harold Kushner and "Holocaust Theology"
   C. God Is Not a "Super-Being"

V. THE NATURE OF EVIL
   A. Evil Is Not a Created Thing
   B. Bringing About a Greater Good
   C. The Atheist's Burden of Proof

VI. GOOD FROM MORAL EVIL
   A. Moral vs. Natural Evil
   B. The Good of Freedom

## LESSON FOUR
# *PROVIDENCE AND THE PROBLEM OF EVIL*

In our last lesson, we learned that because God is infinite, he is not limited in any way. Nothing escapes God's knowledge, his love, or his almighty power. However, when we say this, skeptics might object that the existence of evil, suffering, and randomness in the world contradict God's infinite perfection. How can an all-powerful, all-loving God exist if bad things happen to good people for what appears to be no reason at all? Where is God among the seemingly random events of life? In this lesson, we will investigate two issues that spawn questions like these—providence and the problem of evil.

## THE NATURE OF PROVIDENCE

On August 4, 2013, 19-year-old Katie Lentz left her parent's home in Quincy, Illinois, for Jefferson City, Missouri, where she had a summer internship. While passing through a secluded patch of highway near the town of Center, an oncoming car crossed the center lane and struck Katie's vehicle. Her car was reduced to a mangled pile of metal from which emergency workers struggled to free her. While trapped, Lentz asked for someone to pray with her, and almost instantly a bystander's voice responded, "I will." The bystander turned out to be a Catholic priest who prayed with Katie and anointed her with oil.

After ministering to Katie, the priest stepped aside and prayed while the rescue personnel struggled to free Katie from the wreckage. After several minutes, the responder's tools began to work again and the wreckage became much easier to dismantle. After Katie was freed, several bystanders sought out the priest but he was nowhere to be found.

He had seemingly disappeared without a trace—neither being recognized by anyone at the scene or even appearing in any photographs taken there. These odd coincidences led some media outlets to call the story "a miracle" and even went as far as to entertain the possibility that the priest was actually an angel. However, it was later revealed that the priest was Fr. Patrick Dowling, a cleric who served in the Jefferson City Diocese that included Center, Missouri. While this may not have been a miracle, it was a classic example of another way God interacts with the world through his providence.

A miracle occurs when God intervenes in the world and causes an event to happen that has no natural explanation. Christ's resurrection or the parting of the Red Sea would be examples of events that have supernatural rather than natural causes. Providence, on the other hand, describes how God orders natural causes towards divinely chosen good ends. The First Vatican Council declared:

> By his providence God protects and governs all things which he has made, "reaching mightily from one end of the earth to the other, and ordering all things well." For "all are open and laid bare to his eyes," even those things which are yet to come into existence through the free action of creatures.[46]

Providence is an example of God's perfect knowledge and timing. In the case of Katie and Fr. Dowling, if a different priest at the parish near Katie hadn't fallen ill, then Fr. Dowling would not have volunteered to travel through the rural area where Katie had her accident. Through an innumerable series of natural causes that happened in just the right order, God's perfect timing, or his providence, was made manifest. In an interview about the case, the Vicar of Vocations for the Diocese of Charleston, Fr. Jeffrey Kirby, said:

> [T]he two great gifts that God gives us that are associated with his providence are time and place. To be at the right place at the right time in order to be of service to others is a clear act of God's presence among us. To bring all those pieces together at that time and place is truly evidence of God's providential care.[47]

# THE PROBLEM OF PROVIDENCE

But how does God's providence work? One mistaken way of thinking about providential events is to think that God just gets really lucky. He might have created the universe, but everything that happens after that point is simply random, and God is forced to just do his best managing randomness. However, Romans 8:28 tells us that, "in everything God works for good with those who love him, who are called according to his purpose," and Jesus tells us that God is aware of each bird that drops to the ground (Matt 10:29). God providentially guides everything, not just the big things in the universe.

The other mistaken view, endorsed by a school of philosophers in the 17th century known as "Occasionalists," holds that God directly causes everything that happens. From every leaf that falls to the ground to every human act, God directly causes all of it. However, the *Catechism of the Catholic Church* teaches us that "God created man a rational being, conferring on him the dignity of a person who can *initiate and control his own actions*" (CCC 1730, emphasis added). Thus God cannot be said to directly cause everything that happens.

In his *Summa Theologiae*, St. Thomas Aquinas proposed a view of providence that allows God to be the primary cause of all that happens in the world without making him the *only* cause of what happens. Aquinas said that "there are certain intermediaries of God's providence; for He governs things inferior by superior, not on account of any defect in His power, but by reason of the abundance of His goodness; so that the dignity of causality is imparted even to creatures."[48]

What Aquinas means is that while God is capable of causing everything that happens in the world, he grants creatures the dignity of being causes in the world while ordering what creatures do toward God's providential ends. Providence can be difficult for human beings to understand because when we order things to certain ends (like rolling a ball down a hill) we have to physically intervene, since we don't know what exactly will happen. God's knowledge, however, is not limited like ours. God not only knows what will happen, he knows what *would* happen in any given circumstance. God knows what we would freely do in certain situations, or what would happen in any given natural circumstance (such as how the ball would roll down the hill).

With this knowledge, God can order everything as its primary cause, while allowing created beings to act as *secondary* causes. In regards to humans, God does not negate our freedom but, in knowing what we will freely do, he is able to fold our free choices into his providential plan

for his creation (this is what Bishop Barron calls God's "non-competitive causality"). This corresponds to what we learned in the previous lesson: all moments of time are immediately present to God, and because of this God includes each person's free response to his grace in his plan of salvation (CCC 600). The *Catechism* affirms, "With creation, God does not abandon his creatures to themselves. He not only gives them being and existence, but also, and at every moment, upholds and sustains them in being, enables them to act and brings them to their final end" (CCC 301).

✝

# THE PROBLEM OF EVIL

So if everything works towards good, and God sustains everything that exists, doesn't that mean God uses evil for good and even keeps it in existence? How could an all-loving, all-knowing, and all-powerful God do such a thing? We have now come to one of the most powerful arguments for atheism: the problem of evil. The *Catechism* says, "Faith in God the Father Almighty can be put to the test by the experience of evil and suffering. God can sometimes seem to be absent and incapable of stopping evil" (CCC 272).

The 17th-century atheistic philosopher David Hume put it this way: "Is God willing to prevent evil, but not able? Then he is impotent. Is he able, but not willing? Then he is malevolent. Is he both able and willing? Whence then is evil?"[49]

We can articulate Hume's version of the problem of evil in the following logical argument:

1. God is all-powerful, all-knowing, and all-good.

2. An all-powerful, all-knowing, and all-good being would eliminate evil.

3. Evil exists.

Therefore, God does not exist.

How do we answer an argument like this? First, we should affirm the truth of the argument's first premise. As we've already seen, God is the infinite act of being who sustains all of existence, so he is not limited in any way. However, some theologians and philosophers try to answer the problem of evil by saying that evil occurs because God is limited. For example, in his book *When Bad Things Happen to Good People*, Rabbi Harold Kushner denies that God is all-powerful or that he has a providential plan for his creation. Kushner says painful things that happen to us are not "in any way part of some grand design on God's part. . . . We can turn to Him for help in overcoming it, precisely because we can tell ourselves that God is as outraged by it as we are."[50]

In fact, there is an entire field of Jewish thought called "Holocaust theology" that tries to reconcile the existence of a loving God with the horrors of the Nazi holocaust. Many of these thinkers agree with Rabbi Kushner that God hates evil as much as we do, but like us, he can't get rid of it.[51] There is a similar school of thought in Christian circles called "process theology" which denies that God has direct control over the world. Process theologians say that God "persuades" rather than coerces his creation, and so evil exists because persuasion isn't 100% effective.[52]

However, as Catholics, we know that denying God's infinite power is simply not an option. To believe in a God that is limited or imperfect is to only believe in the existence of a "super-being" we might call god. It is not the same as believing in the true God. Even some atheists recognize this. One such atheist, B.C. Johnson, writes, "Such a God, if not dead, is the next thing to it. And a person who believes in such a ghost of a god is practically an atheist. To call such a thing a god would be to strain the meaning of the word."[53]

✝

## THE NATURE OF EVIL

So the first premise of the argument from evil seems to be solid. Can we solve the problem of evil by denying premise three—"Evil exists"? Of all the premises in the argument from evil, this one seems to be the most secure. Unless we are going to become a devotee of an Eastern religion that denies the reality of evil (along with the reality of the external world and even the self), we must admit that evil and suffering do exist. But while it is true that God sustains the existence of all created beings, and it is true that evil exists, it is not true that God sustains evil. That's because evil is not a created thing.

You might be wondering, how can evil exist, then, if it is not something that God created? The answer is that it can exist as a privation, or an absence, of a good that God did create.

Think of rust on a piece of metal or a serial killer's evil desires. Rust and evil desires don't just

float around in space waiting to strike innocent pipes and people. Instead, they are corruptions of good things and they cannot exist without those good things. If there were no metal, there would be no rust. If there were no people, there would be no evil desires. Aquinas said in the *Summa Contra Gentiles* that "there must always continue to be a subject for evil, if evil is to endure. Of course, the subject of evil is the good, and so the good will always endure."[54]

To put it simply, evil can always mock the good, but it can't defeat it. There must always be some good, even basic goods like existence or freedom, in order for evil to exist. Take away all the good things in the world and you wouldn't have pure evil, you'd have pure nothingness!

Now, think of the argument we examined, especially premise two, "An all-powerful, all-knowing, and all-good being would eliminate evil on earth." One way for God to eliminate all evil would be for him to eliminate all of existence. God could just will every created thing into non-existence, and there would no longer be pain, suffering, or any kind of evil.

Even if God simply willed the non-existence of rational creatures like humans or angels, there would be much less suffering and no moral evil of any kind. Of course, the price paid in getting rid of evil this way may simply be too high. Perhaps some evils are worth enduring for the goods that they parasitically feed upon. Aquinas made this precise point, saying, "God allows evils to happen in order to bring a greater good therefrom."[55]

We can now see how this formulation of the problem of evil fails: the second premise is false. God might not eliminate the evil we currently observe because he can bring a greater good from that evil. Therefore, an atheist must refute this possibility and thus reformulate the argument in this way:

1. God is all-powerful, all-knowing, and all-good.

2. An all-powerful, all-knowing, and all-good being would eliminate evil *because he has no good reason to allow evil to exist.*

3. Evil exists.

Therefore, God does not exist.

With this modified premise it becomes much more difficult, if not impossible, for the atheist to defend the problem of evil. Remember, the problem of evil is an atheistic argument for the non-existence of God, so the burden falls on the atheist to show that his argument proves God does not exist. Too often, the burden of proof gets shifted and the atheist will say to the believer, "Explain to me how God can exist when there's so much evil and suffering." The theist then struggles to explain why God allows certain evils while forgetting that it was the atheist who made an extraordinary claim. He implicitly argued that God and evil are logically incompatible, or that both can't exist at the same time. But why should we believe that's true?

The atheist might simply respond, "Because if God existed he would eliminate evil" but this neglects our reformulation of premise two, "An all-powerful, all-knowing, and all-good being would eliminate evil *because he has no good reason to allow evil to exist.*" The atheist now has to prove that crucial qualifying statement. He has the burden of justifying the claim that God could not possibly have any good reason to allow evil to exist. But as we will see, this is a burden that the atheist simply cannot meet.

✝

## GOOD FROM MORAL EVIL

What might be some of the reasons for God to allow evil? Before we examine those reasons, we must first distinguish between two kinds of evils: the moral and the natural. Moral evil occurs when a rational being, such as a human, acts against the good. For example, animals might kill or forcibly copulate with one another, but only humans can murder or rape. That's because humans can reason and know these acts are wrong. They can surpass animals in knowing that they must not do some acts even if some kind of benefit can be derived from those acts.

One of the goods that can come from God allowing moral evil is freedom, or rational creatures being able to freely choose the good even if that choice is very difficult. St. Augustine once wrote, "For a runaway horse is better than a stone that stays in the right place only because it has no movement or perception of its own; and in the same way, a creature that sins by free will is more excellent than one that does not sin only because it has no free will."[56]

Just as a world with runaway animals is better than a lifeless world of rocks, a world of people who sometimes run away from the good is better than a lifeless world of robots who unthinkingly follow God's commands. As the *Catechism* says,

Angels and men, as intelligent and free creatures, have to journey toward their ultimate destinies by their free choice and preferential love. They can therefore go astray. Indeed, they have sinned. Thus has moral evil, incommensurably more harmful than physical evil, entered the world. God is in no way, directly or indirectly, the cause of moral evil. He permits it, however, because he respects the freedom of his creatures and, mysteriously, knows how to derive good from it (CCC 311).

At this point, an atheist might counter that the Bible teaches that God creates evil, quoting the King James Version's translation of Isaiah 45:7 where God says, "I form the light, and create darkness: I make peace, and create evil: I the LORD do all these things." However, Aquinas recognized that the evil described in this verse refers to "the evil of penalty, and not to the evil of fault." In other words, it refers to *natural* or non-moral evils like pain and not to moral faults (the word "penalty" is even derived from the Latin word for pain, *poena*). God does not cause moral evil, but he can cause or permit the existence of pain as a way of bringing about a greater good. That is why the Revised Standard Version, Catholic Edition (RSV-CE), more accurately translates the passage from its original Hebrew as, "I form light and create darkness, I make weal [well-being] and create woe, I am the LORD, who do all these things."

✝

## GOOD FROM PHYSICAL EVIL

An atheist might say that he can understand why God allows moral evil, but why does God allow natural evils like disease, natural disasters, or animal suffering? What good could they possibly serve?

First, the natural sufferings that take place in this world are the inevitable consequence of limited beings interacting with one another. Aquinas uses the example of fire to explain. Fire, upon becoming better and more perfect, limits other things like air or wood in order to exist. Another example might be animals that require the consumption of other physical beings in order to exist. According to the *Catechism*, "God freely willed to create a world 'in a state of journeying' towards its ultimate perfection. In God's plan this process of becoming involves the appearance of certain beings and the disappearance of others, the existence of the more perfect alongside the less perfect, both constructive and destructive forces of nature. With physical good there exists also *physical evil* as long as creation has not reached perfection" (CCC 310).

Of course, we can still ask why God created a world "journeying to perfection" instead of one already there. One reason is that some goods can only be achieved through this journey, not in the destination of perfection. For example, it's impossible for God to make someone courageous without first placing them in danger, or to make someone compassionate if they have not first suffered alongside another. These are just some of the goods that God can bring about from suffering—a suffering that, from our perspective, can seem pointless.

Second, simply because we cannot see a good that God can bring from evil does not prove that such a good does not exist. Just as we cannot see bacteria or other planets with our unaided eyes, we also cannot see the good God can achieve across the globe or centuries into the future through the seemingly random events that take place in the present. All of the people we know and care about were the providential outcome of thousands of years of momentous actions like marriage and childbirth, trivial actions like choosing which bus to take to work, and even natural occurrences like getting sick or being stuck in a snowstorm. It can be overwhelming to contemplate the millions of past events, including occasions of suffering, that ultimately led to the creation of our individual lives, which are now ordered toward eternal life with God. The *Catechism* says,

> We firmly believe that God is master of the world and of its history. But the ways of his providence are often unknown to us. Only at the end, when our partial knowledge ceases, when we see God "face to face," will we fully know the ways by which—even through the dramas of evil and sin—God has guided his creation to that definitive sabbath rest for which he created heaven and earth (CCC 314).

Finally, it's important to know that even non-believing philosophers recognize that, in the words of agnostic scholar Paul Draper, "theists face no serious logical problem of evil."[57] J.L. Mackie, once a popular atheist defender of the problem of evil, even admitted that as a result of the work of contemporary theistic philosophers like Alvin Plantinga, "[W]e can concede that the problem of evil does not, after all, show that the central doctrines of theism are logically inconsistent with one another."[58]

# THE HEART OF THE PROBLEM

Ultimately, the problem of evil is an objection from the heart rather than from the mind. Even if our minds can understand that God did not create evil, that God has good reasons for allowing evil to exist, and that he will eventually conquer it as our world "journeys to perfection," the reality of evil can still be overwhelming. When we lose a loved one to a violent crime or a seemingly random disease, we might lose hope. Rational arguments may seem cold and antiseptic when we just want everything to feel okay again.

The *Catechism* anticipates this natural human response and says that

> Only Christian faith as a whole constitutes the answer to this question: the goodness of creation, the drama of sin and the patient love of God who comes to meet man by his covenants, the redemptive Incarnation of his Son, his gift of the Spirit, his gathering of the Church, the power of the sacraments and his call to a blessed life to which free creatures are invited to consent in advance, but from which, by a terrible mystery, they can also turn away in advance. *There is not a single aspect of the Christian message that is not in part an answer to the question of evil* (CCC 309).

One of the ways the Christian message answers the problem of evil is that it provides what human beings desire the most when they suffer—meaning.

Victor Frankl was an Austrian psychiatrist who languished for three years in various Nazi concentration camps. After being liberated, Frankl developed a kind of therapy called *logotherapy* to help people cope with difficult life problems. For example, Frankl once counseled a man who was experiencing severe depression after the death of his wife. Frankl's approach to the man's depression was to remind him what would have happened if he had died and his wife had survived him instead. The man saw that through his suffering he was able to spare his wife from the same agonies. His suffering now had meaning. Frankl concludes, "In some way, suffering ceases to be suffering at the moment it finds a meaning, such as the meaning of a sacrifice."[59]

In an atheistic universe there can be no meaning in suffering. As atheist Richard Dawkins puts it, "The universe we observe has precisely the properties we should expect if there is, at bottom, no design, no purpose, no evil and no good, nothing but blind, pitiless indifference."[60] However, if God exists and is all-powerful, then he can provide meaning in our suffering, even if we can't see that meaning in the midst of suffering. One source of meaning is that through our suffering, we can attain grace for other people. Colossians 1:24 says, "Now I rejoice in my sufferings for your sake . . . for the sake of his body, that is, the church."

God, in his mercy, allows our sufferings to be united to Christ's sufferings, so that we too can attain grace for other people, humbly imitating Christ's redemption of all through his perfect act of sacrifice. Pope St. John Paul II, who was accustomed to suffering from Parkinson's disease, reflected on this in his apostolic letter *Salvifici Doloris* (On the Christian Meaning of Human Suffering). He wrote:

> Man hears Christ's saving answer as he himself gradually becomes a sharer in the sufferings of Christ. The answer that comes through this sharing, by way of the interior encounter with the Master, is in itself something more than the mere abstract answer to the question about the meaning of suffering. For it is above all a call. It is a vocation. Christ does not explain in the abstract the reasons for suffering, but before all else he says: "Follow me! Come! Take part through your suffering in this work of saving the world, a salvation achieved through my suffering! Through my cross." Gradually, as the individual takes up his cross, spiritually uniting himself to the cross of Christ, the salvific meaning of suffering is revealed before him.[61]

This is why in the next lesson we will examine what makes the God of the Christian faith different from every other deity—the fact that God became man in the form of Jesus Christ in order to suffer and atone for the sins of the world.

# QUESTIONS FOR UNDERSTANDING

1. What is providence? What are two false views of providence and what is the true view articulated by St. Thomas Aquinas? (Rom 8:28, Matt 10:28-31, CCC 302-308)

2. What is the "argument from evil"? What are some unacceptable ways of resolving the problem of evil? (CCC 272-274, CCC 309)

3. What is the nature of evil? What hidden premise is left out of the argument from evil that severely weakens it? Finally, how do the ideas of greater goods and limited human understanding help us answer the problem of evil? (Gen 50:20, Is 55:8-9, Rom 8:28, Rom 12:21, CCC 310-311)

4. In what ways does the Christian faith help us answer the problem of evil? (John 16:33, Rom 8:28, Col 1:24, 2 Cor 1:3-5, 1 Pet 5:7, CCC 312-314)

# QUESTIONS FOR APPLICATION

1. What events in my life can I attribute to God's providence that ultimately led me closer to God?

2. What particular evil or suffering do I endure in life that makes it difficult to trust in God's goodness? How can I respond more positively to these trials?

3. St. Paul said in 2 Corinthians 1:4 that God "comforts us in all our affliction, so that we may be able to comfort those who are in any affliction, with the comfort with which we ourselves are comforted by God." How do I comfort others when they are suffering? How can I be a better witness of Christ's love to those who are suffering?

# THE MYSTERY
## OF GOD

WORD
on FIRE

# EXPLORING THE TRINITY
## LESSON FIVE OUTLINE

I.     INTRODUCTION
       A.   C.S. Lewis and *Mere Christianity*
       B.   The Divinity of Christ

II.    THE CLAIMS OF CHRIST
       A.   Jesus vs. Socrates, Confucius, and Buddha

III.   "YOUR SINS ARE FORGIVEN"
       A.   Mark 2 and Paralytic on Mat
       B.   Who Can Forgive Sins But God Alone?
       C.   Yom Kippur
       D.   Authority to Change the Torah
       E.   Healing on the Sabbath

IV.   "BEFORE ABRAHAM WAS, I AM"
       A.   Claiming the Divine Name
       B.   Pope Benedict XVI and the *Tetragrammaton*

V.     "DESTROY THIS TEMPLE AND IN THREE DAYS I WILL RAISE IT UP"
       A.   The Death of Jesus
       B.   The Resurrection

VI.   "MY LORD AND MY GOD"
       A.   Doubting Thomas
       B.   Paul, Barnabas, and False Gods

VII.   "THE NAME ABOVE ALL NAMES"
       A.   The Conversion of Saul
       B.   Hymn in Philippians 2
       C.   Humility of Christ
       D.   Jesus Christ is Lord

VIII.    THE EARLY CHURCH – "JESUS CHRIST, OUR GOD"
    A.    Dan Brown's *The Da Vinci Code*
    B.    The Council of Nicaea
    C.    Early Church on the Divinity of Christ
    D.    Early Pagans on Divinity of Christ

IX.    THE DOCTRINE DEFENDED
    A.    Person vs. Nature
    B.    Hypostatic Union
    C.    Two Natures
    D.    Docetist Heresy
    E.    Council of Chalcedon

## LESSON FIVE

# *EXPLORING THE TRINITY*

In the previous lessons we saw how modern people often reduce God from perfect and infinite being to just a kind of super-creature. The same thing happens to Jesus, who, instead of being revered as *ipsum esse* incarnate (God become man), is reduced to the status of an inspiring teacher. In his book *Mere Christianity*, C.S. Lewis argued against this view:

> A man who was merely a man and said the sort of things Jesus said would not be a great moral teacher. He would either be a lunatic—on the level with the man who says he is a poached egg—or else he would be the Devil of Hell. You must make your choice. Either this man was, and is, the Son of God, or else a madman or something worse. You can shut him up for a fool, you can spit at him and kill him as a demon or you can fall at his feet and call him Lord and God, but let us not come with any patronizing nonsense about his being a great human teacher. He has not left that open to us. He did not intend to.[62]

In this lesson, we will examine the biblical and historical evidence for the divinity of Christ, the belief that "Jesus is inseparably true God and true man. He is truly the Son of God who, without ceasing to be God and Lord, became a man and our brother" (CCC 469).

†

## THE CLAIMS OF CHRIST

Karl Jaspers, the famous psychologist and philosopher, described Jesus Christ as one of four "paradigmatic individuals" who radically changed civilization (the others were Socrates, Confucius, and Buddha). However, Jesus' claims and deeds dramatically differed from those of all other wise and influential men.

For example, Buddha said, "Therefore, be ye lamps unto yourselves, be a refuge to yourselves. Hold fast to Truth as a lamp; hold fast to the truth as a refuge."[63] Christ, on the other hand, said, "I am the light of the world; he who follows me will not walk in darkness, but will have the light of life." Socrates said, "I do not fancy I know what I do not know,"[64] while Jesus said, "I am the way, and the truth, and the life; no one comes to the Father, but by me" (John 14:6, cf. John 8:12).

Let's examine some of the other claims Christ made, as well the central miracles that vindicated his divine status.

✝

## "YOUR SINS ARE FORGIVEN"

The atheist Richard Dawkins wrote in his bestselling book, *The God Delusion*, "[T]here is no good historical evidence that [Jesus] ever thought he was divine."[65] Critics who make this claim usually discount Jesus' explicit affirmations of divinity recorded in the Gospel of John as late, legendary developments. They contend that the earliest Gospels only depict Jesus claiming to be a teacher or prophet. However, when we look at even the earliest Gospel accounts of Jesus' life, we find several occasions where Jesus' words and deeds implicitly reveal his divinity.

For example, in Mark 2 we read about a crippled man whose friends bring him to Jesus. Since they are unable to get past the crowd at the door, they cut a hole in the house's roof and lower their friend down to Jesus on a mat. When Jesus sees their faith, he says to the paralytic, "My son, your sins are forgiven" (Mark 2:5).

What makes this simple claim so audacious is that forgiveness can only involve the offended and offending party. For example, imagine you told me that you feel awful about knocking over your neighbor's mailbox with your car. Then I replied, "Don't worry, I forgive you." That wouldn't make sense because the fault involved in breaking the mailbox had nothing to do with me; it only involved you and your neighbor.

Likewise, sin is an offense against God not because it hurts God (nothing can harm *ipsum esse*), but because it harms the humans created in God's image, humans whom God loves and cares about. Sin also harms ourselves, because through our sins we push ourselves away from God and his perfect goodness. The result? Paul tells us that "the wages of sin is death" (Rom 6:23). Sin alienates us from God, which means the only person who can restore us to a loving relationship with God, or forgive us of our sins, is God himself. That's why the scribes said in their hearts, after Jesus forgave the paralytic, "Why does this man speak thus? It is blasphemy! Who can forgive sins but God alone?" (Mark 2:7).

In ancient Israel, the only way one could receive forgiveness of sins was through Yom Kippur. On that day every year, the high priest would enter the Holy of Holies in the Temple in Jerusalem and offer sacrifice to atone for the sins of all Jews. Even during this sacred event, it wasn't the high priest who forgave people's sins—it was God. This brings us back to Jesus' statement in Mark 2:5. The *Catechism* says that by forgiving sins,

> Jesus placed the religious authorities of Israel on the horns of a dilemma. Were they not entitled to demand in consternation, "Who can forgive sins but God alone?" By forgiving sins Jesus either is blaspheming as a man who made himself God's equal or is speaking the truth, and his person really does make present and reveal God's name (CCC 589).

Finally, to show that he really did have authority to forgive sins, and wasn't just a mentally unstable person, Jesus told the paralytic, "I say to you, rise, take up your pallet and go home" (Mark 2:11).

Along with claiming to have the authority to forgive sins, Jesus revealed his divine status when he claimed to have the authority to change the Torah, the sacred law that God had given to Moses. Only a rabbi, or teacher of the law, could interpret this law, and he usually supported his interpretation with the opinions of eminent rabbis who had taught before him. Jesus, however, relied on his own authority to interpret and even change the law.

One prominent example of this was when Jesus chose to heal on the Sabbath (Mark 3:1-6, John 5:1-47). God's law forbade work on the Sabbath (Exod 35:2), but what exactly counted as "work" was a matter of interpretation within rabbinic circles, even up to the present day. The Pharisees claimed that healing, even through the use of a miracle, counted as work and was forbidden, but Jesus rejected that interpretation and chose to heal on the Sabbath.

When the Jewish leaders asked Jesus what authority he had to heal on the Sabbath, he appealed to his relationship with the authority behind the law. He said, "My Father is working still, and I am working" (John 5:17). If Jesus' Father, God, can still be working on the Sabbath, then why can't the Son be working? John 5:18 describes how this answer was received: "The Jews sought all the more to kill him, because he not only broke the Sabbath but also called God his Father, making himself equal with God."

†

## "BEFORE ABRAHAM WAS, I AM"

In the eighth chapter of John's gospel, Jesus revealed to his Jewish audience more details about the relationship he had with "his Father," how Jesus' word would set them free, and how he would save them from death. But Jesus' audience would have none of this, clinging to their tradition. They replied, "Abraham died, as did the prophets; and you say, 'If any one keeps my word, he will never taste death.' Are you greater than our father Abraham, who died? And the prophets died! Who do you claim to be?" Jesus responded, "Your father Abraham rejoiced that he was to see my day; he saw it and was glad" (John 8:52-56).

To this rather cryptic answer, the Jews said, "You are not yet fifty years old, and have you seen Abraham?" Then Jesus dropped a bombshell by saying, "Truly, truly, I say to you, before Abraham was, I AM" (John 8:58). John then tells us what happened: "They took up stones to throw at him; but Jesus hid himself, and went out of the temple."

Why did the Jewish leaders try to stone Jesus for what he said?

Recall in Lesson Three how we learned that God revealed his sacred name to be "I AM." In Hebrew this phrase is *Eyeh Asher Eyeh*, which was abbreviated and came to be known as the *tetragrammaton*, or YHWH. While the original pronunciation has been lost, most Jewish scholars believe God's sacred name was pronounced Yahweh. Part of the reason this pronunciation has been lost was that, out of fear of breaking the second commandment (taking God's name in vain), ancient Jews did not utter the *tetragrammaton*. When this word appeared in scripture, they substituted the Hebrew word for "my Lord" or *adonai*. Even today orthodox Jews spell the word God "G-d" out of reverence for God's name, not daring to write or speak it.

The name of God is so sacred that, at the prompting of Pope Benedict XVI, the Congregation for Divine Worship and the Discipline of the Sacraments released a 2008 directive that prohibited the name Yahweh from being used in Catholic liturgical music. The letter reminded readers that from the beginning of Church history "the sacred *tetragrammaton* was never pronounced in the Christian context nor translated into any of the languages into which the Bible was translated."[66]

The fact that Jesus not only said the divine name, but also claimed it as his own name, was irrefutable proof to his audience that he was a blasphemer worthy of death. The *Catechism* says of statements like this one that

> Only the divine identity of Jesus' person can justify so absolute a claim as "He who is not with me is against me"; and his saying that there was in him "something greater than Jonah, . . . greater than Solomon," something "greater than the Temple"; his reminder that David had called the Messiah his Lord, and his affirmations, "Before Abraham was, I AM" (CCC 590).

✝

## "DESTROY THIS TEMPLE AND IN THREE DAYS I WILL RAISE IT UP"

As Bishop Barron tells us, the week of Jesus' passion reveals how the Son went from his glorious existence with the Father to a shameful death on the cross. But how could Jesus be God if he died on a cross? Isn't it impossible for God to die? It is impossible for God to go out of existence, but that is not the same thing as dying. Death is simply the result of a living creature being reduced to its component parts. In humans, this takes place when our immortal souls separate from our bodies. The end result of this separation is a body that becomes a decomposing corpse. Since Jesus is God, everything he does is an expression of God's actions, which includes dying on the cross. Of course, God did not cease to be, but God's human body separated from his human soul, which resulted in the death of Jesus, the God-man. As the *Catechism* says, "The Son of God therefore communicates to his humanity his own personal mode of existence in the Trinity. In his soul as in his body, Christ thus expresses humanly the divine ways of the Trinity" (CCC 470).

So, God the Son died on a cross in order to atone for the sins of the world. From the perspective of the apostles the situation appeared to be hopeless, as all they saw was their mortal teacher suffering in agony and then breathing his last. Perhaps Jesus' miracles and teachings only meant that he was Elijah or another prophet, as some people believed (Matt 16:14)—that he was just a mortal prophet who had now suffered a violent end like many of the other prophets (Matt 23:30-31).

Of course, Jesus had predicted he would rise from the dead, but the apostles did not know what Jesus meant when he said this (Mark 9:32). Perhaps Jesus meant he would rise at the end of the world, as Martha believed would happen to her brother Lazarus (John 11:24). Jesus did not mean this, and Christ's resurrection from the dead vindicated his status as the only begotten Son of God. Paul writes in Romans 1:4 that Christ was "designated Son of God in power according to the Spirit of holiness by his resurrection from the dead." Peter preached in Jerusalem, "This Jesus God raised up, and of that we all are witnesses. . . . Let all the house of Israel therefore know assuredly that God has made him both Lord and Christ, this Jesus whom you crucified" (Acts 2:32, 36).

The *Catechism* affirms this point:

> Christ's Resurrection is an object of faith in that it is a transcendent intervention of God himself in creation and history. In it the three divine persons act together as one, and manifest their own proper characteristics. The Father's power "raised up" Christ his Son and by doing so perfectly introduced his Son's humanity, including his body, into the Trinity. Jesus is conclusively revealed as "Son of God in power according to the Spirit of holiness by his Resurrection from the dead" (CCC 648).

As Bishop Barron reminds us, in the resurrection of Christ we don't just see a "physical anomaly" or a "fluke of nature." Instead, we see God, who is love itself, manifesting that love in the form of all three members of the Holy Trinity, raising Jesus to glorious, immortal life.

+

# "MY LORD AND MY GOD"

Most of us are familiar with the story of "doubting Thomas." After his resurrection, Jesus appeared to the apostles but one of them, Thomas, was not present. When the other apostles told Thomas about Jesus' appearance, he scoffed, "Unless I see in his hands the print of the nails, and place my finger in the mark of the nails, and place my hand in his side, I will not believe" (John 20:25). Then, Jesus appeared to the apostles and said, "Peace be with you." He invited Thomas to examine his wounds, but the text never mentions Thomas doing that. Instead, Thomas seemed completely convinced that Jesus has risen from the dead and simply declares, "My Lord and my God!" (John 20:28).

In the other scripture verses we've reviewed, Jesus' divinity is revealed in what he says, but here his divinity is made evident in what he does *not* say. For example, Acts 14 describes how Paul and Barnabas were mistaken for the Greek gods Zeus and Hermes. When the citizens of Athens began to worship them, the two men tore their garments and said in anguish, "Men, why are you doing this? We also are men, of like nature with you, and bring you good news, that you should turn from these vain things to a living God who made the heaven and the earth and the sea and all that is in them" (Acts 14:15). In Revelation 19:10, an angel tells John not to worship him, and Acts 12:21-23 describes how Herod Agrippa died because he accepted worship instead of directing that praise to the true God.

Paul, Barnabas, and the angel in heaven wanted to urgently stop blasphemous worship of themselves. Jesus, however, did not do that, because he rightfully deserves worship, since he truly is our Lord and our God.

+

# "THE NAME ABOVE ALL NAMES"

Before he became an apostle, Saul of Tarsus was a Pharisee who ruthlessly persecuted the Christian Church (1 Cor 15:9, Gal 1:13). However, after an encounter with the risen Jesus on the road to Damascus, Saul came to accept the Christian faith (Acts 9). What is remarkable about Paul's testimony is that, despite his fiercely monotheistic upbringing as a Pharisee, Paul

described Jesus in ways that were reserved for God himself. Paul used terms and descriptions that to the Jews were at the least scandalous, and at the most damnable heresies. In his letter to the Philippians, Paul quotes a hymn that describes Jesus' descent from divine glory, his death on the cross, and his restoration to divine glory. He writes:

> Christ Jesus, who, though he was in the form of God, did not count equality with God a thing to be grasped, but emptied himself, taking the form of a servant, being born in the likeness of men. And being found in human form he humbled himself and became obedient unto death, even death on a cross. Therefore God has highly exalted him and bestowed on him the name which is above every name, that at the name of Jesus every knee should bow, in heaven and on earth and under the earth, and every tongue confess that Jesus Christ is Lord, to the glory of God the Father (Phil 2:6-11).

Two striking themes should be noted in this passage of scripture. First, there is the theme of humility. Christ lowered himself to a status that was not originally his own. Christ was not a being who wanted to become divine, such as Adam, who gave into the serpent's temptation to eat the fruit and be "like God." Instead, Christ suppressed the divine glory that was truly his own and humbled himself to become man.

Secondly, as Bishop Barron points out, St. Paul bestows upon Jesus, the man who used to be a carpenter in Galilee, the name that is above all names. Remember that God's name was so sacred that the Jewish people used the title Lord, or *adonai*, instead. Paul boldly says, "Jesus Christ is Lord!"—not that Jesus is with the Lord after the resurrection or that Jesus serves the Lord. Jesus now possesses the name above all names, the very name of God, because he is the God-man.

✝

## THE EARLY CHURCH – "JESUS CHRIST, OUR GOD"

In Dan Brown's bestselling 2003 novel *The Da Vinci Code*, a character named

Sir Leigh Teabing, a historian, tries to set the record straight about who the real Jesus was. He says, "Jesus was viewed by his followers as a mortal prophet . . . a great and powerful man, but a man nonetheless. A mortal."[67] According to him, and many like-minded skeptics, Jesus' divinity was not a doctrine of the Church until Emperor Constantine declared it at the Council of Nicaea in A.D. 325.

But we have plenty of evidence that Christians believed in the divinity of Christ long before Nicaea. In A.D. 177, Melito, the bishop of Sardis (an area that is now occupied by western Turkey), wrote a defense of the faith. He declared that: "born as a son, led forth as a lamb, sacrificed as a sheep, buried as a man, [Jesus] rose from the dead as a God, for he was by nature God and man."[68] In A.D. 155, Justin Martyr referred to Jesus as "a Son; who also, being the first-begotten Word of God, is even God."[69] In the year A.D. 110, St. Ignatius of Antioch began his letter to the Church at Rome by saying, "[T]o the Church beloved and enlightened after the love of Jesus Christ, our God, by the will of him that has willed everything which is."[70] Another Christian writer at that time named Aristides wrote, "God came down from heaven, and from a Hebrew virgin assumed and clothed himself with flesh; and the Son of God lived in a daughter of man."[71]

Evidence that early Christians worshipped Jesus also comes to us from pagans who were either indifferent or hostile to the fledgling faith. The 2nd-century satirist Lucian of Samosata said that Christians worshipped a "crucified sophist."[72] In the year A.D. 112, the governor of Bithynia, Pliny the Younger, wrote to the Roman Emperor Trajan, describing Christians in this way:

> They were accustomed to meet on a fixed day before dawn and sing responsively a hymn to Christ *as to a god* [emphasis added], and to bind themselves by oath, not to some crime, but not to commit fraud, theft, or adultery, not falsify their trust, nor to refuse to return a trust when called upon to do so.[73]

As we can see, there is abundant evidence that the divinity of Christ was a core doctrine of the Church from the earliest period of post-apostolic history. It was not a legend imposed on the Church centuries later by Roman emperors, as critics like Dan Brown claim.

✝

## THE DOCTRINE DEFENDED

What does it mean for Christ to be both God and man? Isn't that contradictory? It's not if we

understand that a person differs from a nature. "Person" refers to relations, or *who* someone is, while "nature" refers to essence, or *what* someone is. So, for example, Michael the Archangel is a person (his "who" is Michael) and he has an angelic nature (his "what" is a rational, immaterial being). Socrates on the other hand, is a person with a human nature—his "what" is a rational being with a material body.

But now we turn to God. The doctrine that God became man is called *the hypostatic union*. It teaches that prior to the Incarnation, God the Son was one divine person (his "who" is the Son) with one divine nature (his "what" is God). Upon becoming incarnate, God the Son assumed a human nature as the man Jesus, or a second "what," which in this case is "human." However, nothing in the divine person or the divine nature of the Son changed during this process. God the Son now possessed two natures, one fully divine and the other fully human. The *Catechism* puts it this way:

> The unique and altogether singular event of the Incarnation of the Son of God does not mean that Jesus Christ is part God and part man, nor does it imply that he is the result of a confused mixture of the divine and the human. He became truly man while remaining truly God. Jesus Christ is true God and true man. During the first centuries, the Church had to defend and clarify this truth of faith against the heresies that falsified it (CCC 464).

These heresies took a variety of forms over the centuries but, unlike modern heresies that deny that Christ is God, these early heresies typically denied that Christ was a man. One of the earliest was Docetism, which taught that Christ was fully God and only appeared to be a man. Christ's human body was simply a costume that the Son wore during his incarnation, and he never experienced a truly human life. St. Ignatius of Antioch gave this biting critique of the Docetists: "He suffered truly, even as also He truly raised up Himself, not, as certain unbelievers maintain, that He only seemed to suffer, as they themselves only seem to be [Christians]."[74]

Other heretics agreed that Christ had a real human body, but they claimed that Christ did not have a human soul or a human mind. They believed that the Son's divinity would have swallowed up the immaterial aspects of Christ's humanity, like his human mind. Fortunately, these errors were officially rebuked at the ecumenical councils at Ephesus and Chalcedon in the 5th century. The Council of Chalcedon eloquently stated the Christology that all Christians must believe as follows:

> [F]ollowing the holy Fathers, all with one consent, teach men to confess one and the same Son, our Lord Jesus Christ, the same perfect in Godhead and also perfect in manhood; truly God and truly man . . . born of the Virgin Mary, the Mother of God, according to the Manhood; one and the same Christ, Son, Lord, Only-begotten, to be acknowledged in two natures, *inconfusedly, unchangeably, indivisibly, inseparably* the distinction of natures being by no means taken away by the union . . . not parted or divided into two persons, but one and the same Son, and only begotten, God the Word, the Lord Jesus Christ.[75]

## QUESTIONS FOR UNDERSTANDING

1. How were Jesus' claims to be able to forgive sin and alter the Sabbath law implicit revelations of his divinity? (Mark 2:1-12, John 5:10-18, John 20:19-23, CCC 580, 589-591)

2.  How were Jesus' actions in John 8:58 and John 20:28 explicit revelations of his divinity? Describe the primary miracle that vindicated Jesus' divine claims. (Acts 12:20-23, 14:15, CCC 640, 643, 651-653)

3.  What historical evidence is there that Christians worshipped Jesus as true God and true man? Include examples from both Christian sources (e.g., Philippians 2, the Church Fathers) and non-Christian sources.

4.  What is the difference between a person and a nature? Use these terms to describe the hypostatic union, the doctrine that God became man.

## QUESTIONS FOR APPLICATION

1.  When I pray to God, what or who do I envision? How can I cultivate a more intimate relationship with Jesus as the divine person with two natures?

2. Reflect on the beauty and unprecedented event that took place when *ipsum esse* became an unborn child, who lived within the womb of Mary. How can devotion to Mary help me better understand who Jesus really is?

3. How can I better share the truth about who Jesus is to non-Christian friends or family? What steps can I take to improve my confidence in proclaiming "the only name under which we are saved" (Acts 4:12)?

# THE MYSTERY
## OF GOD

WORD
on FIRE

# THE GOD WHO IS LOVE
## LESSON SIX OUTLINE

I.  INTRODUCTION
    A. The Central Mystery of Faith

II.  THEOLOGICAL NONSENSE?
    A. Richard Dawkins and *The God Delusion*
    B. Technical Terms
    C. Being
    D. Person
    E. Nature

III.  THE DOGMA OF THE TRINITY
    A. One God in Three Persons
    B. The Holy Spirit is God
    C. Three Distinct Persons
    D. St. Patrick's Analogy of the Trinity
    E. Athanasian Creed

IV.  TRINITARIAN HERESIES
    A. Modalism
    B. Arianism

V.  ST. AUGUSTINE: MIND AS IMAGE OF THE TRINITY
    A. Analogy from *De Trinitate*
    B. Self-Knowledge
    C. Self-Love

VI.  AQUINAS: TRINITY WITHIN SIMPLICITY
    A. St. Thomas Aquinas and the Chain of Being
    B. Distinction vs. Division

VII.   RATZINGER: TRINITY AS ABSOLUTE RELATIVITY
   A.  Joseph Ratzinger (Pope Benedict XVI)
   B.  *Introduction to Christianity*
   C.  Principle of Relatedness
   D.  Absolute Relation

## LESSON SIX

# THE GOD WHO IS LOVE

In our study of God, we learned about the reasons to believe in God, God's essential attributes, God's relationship to the world, and how it is possible for God to become a man in the person of Jesus Christ. In our final lesson we will explore what the *Catechism of the Catholic Church* calls "the central mystery of Christian faith and life. It is the mystery of God in himself. It is therefore the source of all the other mysteries of faith, the light that enlightens them. It is the most fundamental and essential teaching in the 'hierarchy of the truths of faith'" (CCC 234).

So what is this central mystery? The answer is the Most Holy Trinity. By "mystery" the *Catechism* does not mean that the Trinity is some unknowable black hole. Instead, the Trinity is something we only know about because God has revealed it to us in many statements Jesus spoke and in the wisdom of the Holy Spirit through the Church. While we will never fully comprehend the Trinity, God has given us the ability to reason, and this allows us to better understand this awe-inspiring mystery that lies at the core of who God is.

## THEOLOGICAL NONSENSE?

In *The God Delusion*, Richard Dawkins says the following of the Trinity:

> Rivers of medieval ink, not to mention blood, have been squandered over the "mystery" of the Trinity, and in suppressing deviations such as the Arian heresy. Arius of Alexandria, in the fourth century AD, denied that Jesus was *consubstantial* (i.e., of the same substance or essence) with God. What on earth could that possibly mean, you are probably asking? Substance? What "substance"? What exactly do you mean by "essence"? "Very little" seems the only reasonable reply.[76]

Dawkins's then quotes the *Catholic Encyclopedia's* definition of the Trinity before curtly dismissing it as having the "characteristically obscurantist flavor of theology."[77]

Now, this is nothing more than an argument from ignorance—saying, "I don't understand it, so it must not be so." But imagine I picked up a copy of Richard Dawkins's bestselling book *The Selfish Gene* and I came across the following passage in it: "Genes are competing directly with their alleles for survival, since their alleles in the gene pool are rivals for their slot on the chromosomes of future generations."[78] What if I said, "What on earth could that possibly mean? Alleles? 'Competing' genes? This whole evolution thing is just nonsense!"

Of course, Dawkins would rightly chide me for dismissing an entire field of thought just because I didn't understand the field's jargon or its technical language. It's expected that non-experts won't understand jargon because the terms were created so that the field's experts (who already know what these words mean) wouldn't have to use long, cumbersome definitions as they discussed the finer points of their research. Just as biologists like Dawkins use technical terms that require explanation, theologians like Augustine and Aquinas did the same. Therefore, knowing the meaning of these terms is crucial when it comes to discussing the Trinity, especially the terms "being," "person," and "nature."

*Being* refers to existence, the fact that something "is." We know that only God *is* being itself, and because of this, there is only one God (Dt 6:4). Within creation, however, there are individual beings like you, me, fish, rocks, or desktop printers that *have* being. These things exist as unified entities, but they are not all alike.

You and I are a kind of being called *persons* because we are relational in nature. Something is a being if it "is," while something is a person if it is a "who." Fish, rocks, and finicky printers are all beings, but they are not persons. Why not?

Here we come to *nature* (also known as "essence"), or "what" a being is. For example, a fish has a nature that lets it swim, a rock has a nature that makes it immobile, and a printer, even though it is a technological artifact and not a natural being, has a nature imposed upon its parts (it's a machine ordered towards copying information onto paper). Persons, like you or me, have a rational nature. We are ordered towards using reason in order to understand ourselves and the world around us. That is why Aristotle defined man as a "rational animal." *Animal* refers to the kind of being we are (i.e., a complex organism) while *rational* describes the kind of nature we have, or what distinguishes us from other complex organisms.

According to Catholic author Frank Sheed,

> Nature answers the question of what we are; person answers the question of who we are. Every being has a nature; of every being we may properly ask, "What is it?" But not every being is a person: only rational beings are persons. We could not properly ask of a stone or a potato or an oyster, "Who is it?"[79]

†

# THE DOGMA OF THE TRINITY

So how does this relate to the Trinity? Put simply, the dogma of the Trinity teaches that God is one being who exists as three persons, Father, Son, and Holy Spirit, each of whom fully possesses the divine nature and is coequal and coeternal with the other persons. According to the *Catechism*, "We do not confess three Gods, but one God in three persons, the 'consubstantial Trinity.' The divine persons do not share the one divinity among themselves but each of them is God whole and entire" (CCC 253).

Just as there are beings that include zero persons (e.g., rocks, fish, printers) and beings that include one person (e.g., you, me, an angel), God is being itself in three divine persons. The Father, Son, and Holy Spirit don't share the divine nature like a blanket pulled in every direction by three uncomfortable people. Instead, each member of the Trinity fully possesses the divine nature—each person is fully God.

Most people agree the Father is fully divine, and in our last lesson we learned that Scripture plainly teaches that the Son is of the same substance, or shares the same divine nature, as his Father. Some people balk, however, at the idea that the Holy Spirit is God. They might think of the Spirit as just a force or energy through which God affects creation. But who else can "guide us into all truth" (John 16:13) or, as Paul says of the Spirit, "comprehend the thoughts of God" (1 Cor 2:11) except for God himself? Moreover, in the Book of Acts, Peter questions Ananias and

says to him, "Ananias, why has Satan filled your heart to lie to the Holy Spirit . . . You have not lied to men but to God" (Acts 5:3-5). Peter's admonishment shows that the Holy Spirit is God.

In order to not be confused we must remember that God is not a *person*, God is *being*, and being is not limited in how many persons it can be. The divine nature is also not limited in how it is manifested, and so it can exist as three divine persons. As Frank Sheed says in his book *Theology and Sanity*:

> [W]e must not say three separate persons, but three distinct persons, because although they are distinct—that is to say, no one of them is either of the others—yet they cannot be separated, for each is what he is by the total possession of the one same nature: apart from that one same nature, no one of the three persons could exist at all. And we must not use any phrase which suggests that the three persons *share* the Divine Nature. For we have seen that in the Infinite there is utter simplicity, there are no parts, therefore no possibility of sharing. The infinite Divine Nature can be possessed only in its totality. In the words of the Fourth Council of the Lateran, "There are three persons indeed, but one utterly simple substance, essence, or nature."[80]

That is why, in spite of how famous it's become, St. Patrick's analogy of the Trinity that compares it to a three-leaf clover is a bad one. Each leaf of the clover only shares in part of the clover, not the whole thing. This analogy leads to tri-theism, or the belief in three limited gods that each contains a part of the divine nature – not one God who exists as three fully divine persons.

A better approach than modern analogies are the ancient creeds, such as the creed which comes from the legacy of St. Athanasius, called the Athanasian Creed. It describes the Trinity in this way:

> We worship one God in Trinity, and Trinity in Unity; neither confounding the persons nor dividing the substance. For there is one person of the Father, another of the Son, and another of the Holy Spirit. But the Godhead of the Father, of the Son, and of the Holy Spirit is all one, the glory equal, the majesty

coeternal. . . . The Father is God, the Son is God, and the Holy Spirit is God; and yet they are not three Gods, but one God. . . . in this Trinity none is afore or after another; none is greater or less than another. But the whole three persons are coeternal, and coequal. So that in all things, as aforesaid, the Unity in Trinity and the Trinity in Unity is to be worshipped.[81]

✝

# TRINITARIAN HERESIES

According to the *Catechism*,

> During the first centuries the Church sought to clarify her Trinitarian faith, both to deepen her own understanding of the faith and to defend it against the errors that were deforming it. This clarification was the work of the early councils, aided by the theological work of the Church Fathers and sustained by the Christian people's sense of the faith. (CCC 250)

For example, one of the earliest heresies about the Trinity was modalism, or as it was known at the time, Sabellianism. It was named after the 2nd-century heretic Sabellius, who tried to reconcile the teaching that there is only one God with the teaching that God is three persons. Sabellius claimed that there is indeed one God, but God manifests himself as the Father at some times, the Son at others, and the Holy Spirit at other times. The Trinity is not made up of three separate persons, but three separate modes through which the one person of God operates.

However, this is a heresy, because, as the Athanasian Creed says, it "confounds the persons." The *Catechism* says that, "'Father', 'Son', 'Holy Spirit' are not simply names designating modalities of the divine being, for they are really distinct from one another" (CCC 254). Scripture demonstrates this, for example, in John 17:5 when Jesus says, "Father, glorify me in your own presence with the glory which I had with you before the world was made." If modalism were true, then Jesus would be talking to himself about how much he enjoyed spending time with himself before he created the world, which is, of course, absurd. This is why we should not compare the Trinity to water that can be a solid, liquid, or gas while remaining $H_2O$, or to a man who can be a father, son, and husband while remaining one person. God is not three roles or *modes*. God is instead three distinct divine persons.

While modalism "confounded the persons," the heresy of Arianism, espoused by the 4th-century bishop Arius, "divided the substance." It reduced the son to a "semi-divine" status because it denied that the Father and the Son are equal in divinity. This is why the Nicene Creed, which was formulated in part as a condemnation of Arianism, affirms that Jesus is, "the Only Begotten Son of God, born of the Father before all ages. God from God, Light from Light, true God from true God, begotten, not made, consubstantial with the Father; through him all things were made."[82]

Now that we understand the Trinity and various heretical views about it, we can peer more deeply into this mystery with the help of three great Catholic thinkers: St. Augustine, St. Thomas Aquinas, and Pope Benedict XVI.

✝

## ST. AUGUSTINE: MIND AS IMAGE OF THE TRINITY

You may have been disappointed to see that many popular analogies used to describe the Trinity (e.g., clover, water) are hopelessly flawed. Does this mean that we should give up trying to explain the Trinity through familiar terms? The 4th-century theologian St. Augustine of Hippo didn't think so, and he offered an analogy of his own in *De Trinitate* (On the Trinity).

Augustine's analogy starts with the concept of the human mind. Augustine believes that we are created in the image and likeness of God, but this image is not related to our physical appearance. God doesn't literally have a human-oid appearance and a fleshy body. Instead our minds mirror God in some small but appreciable way. What way could that be?

One of the unique things about human minds is that they are able to think about themselves. In all other aspects of life the "subject" is distinct from the "object." The tree is not the leaf it grows, and the lion is not the zebra he might be eating. But when we say things like, "Where am I?" or "I'm better than this," we, the subject, investigate ourselves and become the object of our own inquiry. We are able to develop *notitia sui*, or "self-knowledge." Augustine says,

[E]ven our own face itself is out of the reach of our own seeing it; because it is not there where our look can be directed. But when it is said to the mind, "Know yourself"; then it knows itself by that very act by which it understands the word "yourself", and this for no other reason than that it is present to itself.[83]

Augustine says that once the mind becomes fully aware of itself, it begins to love itself. Now, as Bishop Barron points out, this does not mean the mind loves itself like a college student loves pizza or a husband loves his wife. Instead, Augustine means that the mind desires to know itself and will good for itself, as opposed to any other exterior object. He says, "[W]hen the mind knows itself and loves itself, there remains a trinity: mind, love, knowledge; and this trinity is not confounded together by any commingling: although they are each severally in themselves and mutually all in all."[84]

In the human mind, made in the image and likeness of God, we find a faint image of God, a Trinity of three coequal and coeternal divine persons. After all, we don't say that our knowledge is all that matters, nor that we are only our conscious self divorced from any understanding. Likewise, the Father is not a solitary being that only knows the Son from afar, and the Son is not a mere emanation of the Father. Rather, the three persons of the Trinity are completely united and coequal, sacrificing their distinctions just as our mind, knowledge, and will, manifested in self-love, equally coexist but remain distinct from one another.

As one commenter on Augustine puts it,

> There is thus an image of the Trinity: mind, which is akin to the Father; knowledge which is the offspring of mind, and so is akin to the Son; and love which binds the mind with the knowledge it possesses. Just as the Son is not inferior to the father, so knowledge is not inferior to its parent, mind, since they share the same essence. Equally, just as the Holy Spirit is equal to Father and Son, so love permeates both mind and knowledge, uniting itself with both.[85]

✝

## AQUINAS: TRINITY WITHIN SIMPLICITY

Augustine's analogy of the mind is helpful because the mind's production of knowledge does not make it superior to knowledge. We wouldn't say the mind is supreme and its knowledge is irrelevant, nor would we say our knowledge is identical to our minds, since if all our

knowledge was compiled into a gigantic book, that would not be identical to our mind itself. There is still, however, a nagging question. How can God, whom we have taken great pains to describe as existing without any division, be a Trinity?

Here is where St. Thomas Aquinas offers us some helpful insights. Thomas applied Augustine's observations about the mind to what medieval philosophers called *scala naturae*, the great chain of being. This was the idea that everything that exists can be ranked on a scale from less perfect to more perfect based on its possession of "higher-order" properties. So, for example, a plant is more perfect than a stone since it can grow and reproduce, an animal is more perfect than a plant because it can propel itself, and a man is more perfect than a non-rational animal because he can discern where he is propelling himself and choose the wisest course of action.

According to Thomas, as creatures ascend the chain and become more perfect, they gradually gain the ability to form an image of themselves. Bishop Barron uses the examples of a rock crudely forming an "image of itself" when plopping into a patch of soft mud, a plant spawning a seed, or an animal gestating its offspring. Man, however, is able to make the big "metaphysical leap" and create an immaterial image of himself in his own mind.

Of course, this kind of image is still incomplete. As fallen and finite humans, we might think we are better than we really are, or we might fall into despair and think we are worse than we really are. What the angels have over human beings, Aquinas says, is their immaterial intelligence. Our minds are often affected by our bodily states (think of how hard it is to think when you're hungry or tired, for example) but angels are spiritual in nature, so they do not have this problem. Unlike us, they can mentally generate a perfect self-image.

But we have not reached the highest level of the chain of being. While the angels can generate a self-image not dependent on the material world, they still rely on God in order to exist and function. God, however, can generate a perfect interior act of self-replication that depends on no external being in order to exist. This generation, equal to the Father in every way, is the Son. The Son sees the Father from all eternity and the Father sees the Son from all eternity. The two then breathe out their love for each other and this dual procession—or *spiration*, as Thomas calls it—

is the Holy Spirit. But don't we now have three persons existing within what should be simple, undivided being?

No, says Thomas, because a *distinction* is not the same as a *division*. The Father, the Son, and the Holy Spirit are not three separate entities who each share the divine nature. The Council of Florence taught instead that the members of the Trinity fully dwell in one another:

> Because of that unity the Father is wholly in the Son and wholly in the Holy Spirit; the Son is wholly in the Father and wholly in the Holy Spirit; the Holy Spirit is wholly in the Father and wholly in the Son.[86]

Therefore, the only distinction found in the Trinity is the acknowledgement of its relations—not a limit or deficiency in any of its members. According to the *Catechism*, the members of the Trinity "are distinct from one another in their relations of origin: 'It is the Father who generates, the Son who is begotten, and the Holy Spirit who proceeds. . . . While they are called three persons in view of their relations, we believe in one nature or substance'" (CCC 254-255). As Bishop Barron says, we "call" the members of the Trinity persons because that's the closest word we have to describe that they are. But the Father, Son, and Spirit dwell within one another without sacrificing distinction, doing so in a way that creatures simply cannot emulate.

✝

## RATZINGER: TRINITY AS ABSOLUTE RELATIVITY

In his work *Introduction to Christianity*, Cardinal Joseph Ratzinger (later Pope Benedict XVI) says that God possesses all perfections, including the perfections of unity and plurality. This may seem contradictory but Cardinal Ratzinger is not saying that God possesses the perfections of "unity" and "not-unity" at the same time. Instead, God is perfect oneness in his being and perfect otherness in his relations.

Ratzinger writes,

> God as substance, as "being", is absolutely one. If we nevertheless have to speak of him in the category of triplicity, this does not imply any multiplication of substances but means that in the one and indivisible God there exists the phenomenon of dialogue, the reciprocal exchange of word and love in their attachment to each other.[87]

The *Catechism* affirms this point and says, "Because it does not divide the divine unity, the real distinction of the persons from one another resides solely in the relationships which relate them to one another" (CCC 255).

Now, normally the principle of "relatedness" or "relativity" (not to be confused with Einstein's theory known by the same name) entails imperfection. To be related to another means that one is receiving from another what one does not possess. If I am related to the pope by being thousands of miles away from him, and exist to him only as a faint memory of a meeting that took place years ago, then that means I lack the location where he is and more memorable moments with him. If my wife is related to me in a marital way, then she completes what is lacking in me. Through the marital act we become "one flesh," and our bodies are ordered towards a good neither of us can achieve on our own. God, however, is absolute and depends on no one else in order to complete him. For example, God's knowledge and power are not relative to circumstance but are infinite and unconditioned; they depend on nothing and no one else.

What Ratzinger says is that within God even the concept of relation itself is absolute. He writes,

> Here the decisive point comes beautifully to light. "Father" is purely a concept of relationship. Only in being for the other is he Father; in his own being in himself he is simply God. Person is the pure relation of being related, nothing else. Relationship is not something extra added to the person, as it is with us; it only exists at all as relatedness.[88]

The great and wonderful mystery of God is that he is not an unknown being that exists far away "out there." He is being itself, and it is only because of him that we exist and have the ability to freely affect our world and enter into relation with him. But why would God want a relationship with an infinitesimally smaller creature like us? It is because God is love (1 John 4:8), and this description is not a platitudinous metaphor. It expresses the deepest reality of who God is—eternal self-giving relation seen in the Father and the Son, whose perfect love for one another breathes forth the Holy Spirit. God is not an unknown force, or a terrifying, solitary despot eager to impose his will on us. He is the eternal perfection of love within a communion of persons, and it is that love, manifested though the Spirit into our hearts, that provides us with the grace that leads to eternal life.

Let us conclude with this eloquent observation from the *Catechism*:

> "O blessed light, O Trinity and first Unity!" God is eternal blessedness, undying life, unfading light. God is love: Father, Son and Holy Spirit. God freely wills to communicate the glory of his blessed life. Such is the "plan of his loving kindness", conceived by the Father before the foundation of the world, in his beloved Son: "He destined us in love to be his sons" and "to be conformed to the image of his Son", through "the spirit of sonship". This plan is a "grace [which] was given to us in Christ Jesus before the ages began", stemming immediately from Trinitarian love. It unfolds in the work of creation, the whole history of salvation after the fall, and the missions of the Son and the Spirit, which are continued in the mission of the Church. . . .
>
> The ultimate end of the whole divine economy is the entry of God's creatures into the perfect unity of the Blessed Trinity. But even now we are called to be a dwelling for the Most Holy Trinity: "If a man loves me," says the Lord, "he will keep my word, and my Father will love him, and we will come to him, and make our home with him" (CCC 257, 260).

## QUESTIONS FOR UNDERSTANDING

1. Richard Dawkins asks of the Trinity, "Do we have one God in three parts, or three Gods in one?"[89] What is wrong with the two options Dawkins presents, and what is the correct summary of the Trinity? (CCC 253)

2.  What are two common heresies related to the Trinity? (CCC 254-255)

3.  How did St. Augustine think that the human mind resembled the Trinity?

4. What concept do St. Thomas Aquinas and Cardinal Ratzinger use to explain how God can exist as three persons while remaining simple and undivided?

5. How does the concept of the Trinity more fully explain 1 John 4:8, "God is love"?

# QUESTIONS FOR APPLICATION

1. Do I more often conceive of God as a solitary person or as a Trinity of three persons? How can I better relate to each member of the Trinity through prayer?

2. The *Catechism* says, "The Christian family is a communion of persons, a sign and image of the communion of the Father and the Son in the Holy Spirit" (CCC 2205). How can I better model the complete gift of self within my family as God models through the relations in the Trinity?

3. Theology can be difficult to understand, especially the mystery of God. What questions still linger in my mind after this lesson? What commitment will I make to build upon what I have learned so far?

# BIOGRAPHICAL INFORMATION

## MOST REVEREND ROBERT E. BARRON

Bishop Robert Barron is the founder of Word on Fire Catholic Ministries and the host of *CATHOLICISM*, a groundbreaking, award-winning documentary about the Catholic Faith. In July 2015, Pope Francis appointed him auxiliary bishop of the Archdiocese of Los Angeles. He previously served as the Rector-President of Mundelein Seminary/University of St. Mary of the Lake from 2012 until 2015.

Bishop Barron's website, WordOnFire.org, reaches millions of people each year. The site hosts daily blog posts, weekly articles and video commentaries, and an extensive audio archive of homilies. Bishop Barron's homilies are heard by tens of thousands of visitors each week. His regular YouTube videos have been viewed millions of times, and thousands of people receive his daily email reflections during Lent and Advent.

EWTN (The Eternal Word Television Network) and CatholicTV broadcast Bishop Barron's videos and documentaries to a worldwide audience of over 150 million people. His weekly Word on Fire radio program has been broadcast in Chicago (WGN) and throughout the country (Relevant Radio - 950 AM Chicago) to over 30 million listeners.

Bishop Barron is a #1 Amazon bestselling author and has published twelve books and hundreds of essays and articles on theology and the spiritual life. He works with NBC News in New York as an on-air contributor and analyst. He is also a frequent commentator for the *Chicago Tribune, FOX News, CNN, EWTN, Our Sunday Visitor,* the *Catholic Herald* in London, and *Catholic News Agency.*

Bishop Barron's pioneering work in evangelizing through the new media led Francis Cardinal George to describe him as "one of the Church's best messengers." He has keynoted many conferences and events all over the world, including the opening keynote talk at the 2015 World Meeting of Families.

He was appointed to the theological faculty of Mundelein Seminary in 1992, and has also served as a visiting professor at the University of Notre Dame and at the Pontifical University of St. Thomas Aquinas. He was twice scholar in residence at the Pontifical North American College at the Vatican.

Ordained in 1986 in the Archdiocese of Chicago, Bishop Barron received a Master's Degree in Philosophy from the Catholic University of America in 1982 and a doctorate in Sacred Theology from the Institut Catholique de Paris in 1992.

## TRENT HORN

After his conversion to the Catholic faith, Trent Horn pursued an undergraduate degree in history from Arizona State University, and then earned a graduate degree in theology from the Franciscan University of Steubenville. He is currently pursuing a graduate degree in philosophy from Holy Apostles College in Connecticut.

In 2012 Trent joined the staff of Catholic Answers, an organization that is dedicated to explaining and defending the Catholic faith. He currently serves them as a staff apologist and public speaker. Trent is a regular guest on the radio program *Catholic Answers Live* as well as the co-host of the weekly radio show *Hearts and Minds*, broadcast live in the Diocese of San Diego.

Trent is also an accomplished author who has penned dozens of booklets and articles about Catholic apologetics as well as two books, *Answering Atheism* (2013) and *Persuasive Pro-life* (2014), both of which are published by Catholic Answers Press. To learn more about Trent and his work visit his personal website, http://trenthorn.com.

# THE MYSTERY
## OF GOD

# ENDNOTES

# ENDNOTES

## † CHAPTER ONE

1. Richard Dawkins, *The God Delusion*, (New York: Bantam Press, 2006), 1, 5.

2. Unless otherwise noted, all Bible citations come from *Revised Standard Version, 2nd Catholic Edition* (RSV-2CE).

3. Pope Benedict XVI, "Address of His Holiness Benedict XVI at the Meeting for Peace in Assisi," October 27, 2011.

4. Daniel Dennett, "The Bright Stuff," *New York Times*, July 12, 2003.

5. Anselm, *Monologion and Proslogion*, trans. Thomas Williams (Hackett Publishing Company, 1995, original 1076), 121.

6. Rudolf Otto, *The Idea of the Holy*, 2nd edition (London: Oxford University Press, 1958), 12.

7. John Paul II, "The Proofs for God's Existence," Papal Audience, July 10, 1985.

8. Ludwig Feuerbach, *Lectures on the Essence of Religion*, trans. Ralph Mannheim (New York: Harper and Row, 1967), 187.

9. Ludwig Feuerbach, *The Essence of Christianity*, 2nd edition (Mineola, NY: Dover Publications, 2008), 12.

10. Ibid, 39.

11. Christopher Hitchens, *God Is Not Great: How Religion Poisons Everything* (New York: Hachette Book Group, 2007), 213.

12. Thomas Nagel, *The Last Word.* (New York: Oxford University Press, 1997), 130.

13. Peter Kreeft and Ronald K. Tacelli, *Handbook of Catholic Apologetics* (San Francisco: Ignatius Press, 2009), 83-84.

14. Aristotle, *On the Heavens*, Book I, Chapter 4.

15. Augustine, *Confessions*, Book I, Chapter 1.1.

16. Karl Marx, *Contribution to the Critique of Hegel's Philosophy of Right*, Introduction.

17. Jean-Paul Sartre, "Existentialism is a Kind of Humanism," 1946.

## † CHAPTER TWO

18. Edward Feser, *Aquinas: A Beginner's Guide* (Oxford: Oneworld Publications, 2009), 62-63.

19. Richard Dawkins, *The God Delusion* (New York: Bantam Press, 2006) 77.

20. St. Thomas Aquinas, *Summa Theologica*, Second and Revised Edition, trans. Fathers of the English Dominican Province (1920), Introduction.

21. Sir Arthur Conan Doyle, *The Sign of the Four* (London: Penguin Books, 1982), 51.

22. Richard Taylor, *Metaphysics*, 4th ed. (Englewood Cliffs, NJ: Prentice-Hall, 1991), 100-101.

23. Paul Edwards, "The Cosmological Argument," in *Critiques of God*, ed. Peter A. Angeles (Amherst: Prometheus Books, 1997), 51-52.

24. Derek Parfit, *On What Matters: Volume Two* (Oxford: Oxford University Press, 2011), 27.

25. St. Thomas Aquinas, *Summa Contra Gentiles*, trans. Joseph Kenny, O.P. (New York: Hanover House, 1955-57), I.13.30.

26. David Albert, "*On the Origin of Everything: A Universe from Nothing* by Lawrence Krauss," *New York Times*, March 23, 2012.

† CHAPTER THREE

27. Dawkins, *The God Delusion*, 109.

28. Ibid.

29. Fourth Lateran Council, canon 1.

30. The question of how God can be simple while being a Trinity of three persons is addressed at length in lesson six.

31. Dawkins, *The God Delusion*, 149.

32. Richard Swinburne, *The Coherence of Theism* (Oxford: Oxford University Press, 1993) 107.

33. Anselm, *Anselm of Canterbury: The Major Works*, ed. Brian Davies and G.R. Evans (Oxford: Oxford University Press, 2008) 98.

34. Erik Wielenberg, "Dawkins's Gambit, Hume's Aroma, and God's Simplicity," *Philosophia Christi*, Vol. 11, No. 1, 2009.

35. Pontifical Council for Culture & Pontifical Council for Interreligious Dialogue, "Jesus Christ the Bearer of the Water of Life: A Christian Reflection on the 'New Age,'" *L'Osservatore Romano*, August 13/20 2003.

36. *The Shepherd*, 1:1:1.

37. *To Autolycus*, 2:4.

38. It's important to remember that while God is not essentially embodied, he can choose to become embodied, such as when he became the man Jesus Christ. However, this does

not affect his essentially spiritual and immaterial nature. This will be explained in full in lesson five.

39. This common saying has been adapted from what Chaucer originally wrote in Part One of his 1368 work "The Clerk's Tale," part of his *Canterbury Tales*. It reads, "For though we sleep, or wake, or roam, or ride. Time flees away; it nowhere will abide."

40. Augustine, *Confessions*, Book XI, 14.

41. Augustine, *Confessions*, Book XI, 15.

42. However, as C.S. Lewis observed, God is able to enter into time as a man without losing his timeless existence. Lewis likened this to how an author can enter a story he's writing as one of its characters while still transcending and observing all of the events in the book. Granted, this isn't a perfect analogy, but it still helps us see that God is not limited by anything he creates, nor is he isolated from anything he creates. See C.S. Lewis, *Mere Christianity* (New York: HarperOne, 1952) 166-172.

43. Sharon Kaye, *Medieval Philosophy: A Beginner's Guide* (Oxford: Oneworld, 2008) 85-86.

44. Boethius, *The Consolation of Philosophy*, Book V.6, Cited in Aquinas, *Summa Theologiae*, Part I.10.1.

45. Augustine, City of God, Book V, Chapter 10.

## ✝ CHAPTER FOUR

46. First Vatican Council, 1.4.

47. Joseph Pronechen, "Father Patrick Dowling and the 'Missouri Miracle,'" *National Catholic Register*, 08/15/2013. Available online at: http://www. ncregister.com/daily-news/father-patrick-dowling-and-the-missouri-miracle

48. Aquinas, *Summa Theologiae*, I.22.3.

49. David Hume, *Dialogues Concerning Natural Religion* (Millis, MA: Agora Publications, 2004) 119.

50. Harold Kushner, *When Bad Things Happen to Good People* (New York: Anchor Books, 2004) 148.

51. "God wants the righteous to live peaceful, happy lives, but sometimes even he can't bring that about. It is too difficult even for God to keep cruelty and chaos from claiming their innocent victims." Ibid, 59.

52. Process theology has its roots in the thought of Alfred North Whitehead (1861-1947). A brief summary of it can be found in Alister McGrath, *Christian Theology: An Introduction*, 5th edition, (West Sussex: Wiley-Blackwell, 2011) 214-215.

53. B. C. Johnson, *The Atheist Debater's Handbook* (New York: Prometheus Books, 1983) 105.

54. Aquinas, *Summa Contra Gentiles*, III.12.2.

55. Aquinas, *Summa Theologiae*, III.1.3.

56. Augustine, *On Free Choice of the Will* (USA: Hackett Publishing Company, 1993), 81.

57. Paul Draper, "Pain and Pleasure: An Evidential Problem for Theists," *Nous* 23 (1989): 331-350.

58. J. L. Mackie, *The Miracle of Theism: Arguments for and against the Existence of God* (Oxford: Oxford University Press, 1982) 154. See Alvin Plantinga, *God, Freedom, and Evil* (Grand Rapids: Wm. B. Eerdmans Publishing Co, 1977) for his approach to answering the logical problem of evil.

59. Victor Frankl, *Man's Search for Meaning* (New York: Pocket Books, 1984) 135.

60. Dawkins, *River Out of Eden: A Darwinian View of Life* (London: Phoenix, 1996) 133.

61. John Paul II, *Salvifici Doloris*, 26.

## CHAPTER FIVE

62. C. S. Lewis, *Mere Christianity* (London: HarperCollins, 1952) 54.

63. From "The Buddha's Farewell Address," in Paul Carus, *The Gospel of Buddha: Compiled from Ancient Records* (Chicago and London: The Open Court Publishing Company, 1915).

64. Based on a saying recorded in Plato, *Apology* 21d.

65. Dawkins, *The God Delusion*, 109.

66. Francis Cardinal Arinze, "Letter to the Bishop's Conferences on 'The Name of God'" June 29, 2008. Available online at: http://www.usccb.org/prayer-and-worship/the-mass/frequently-asked-questions/upload/name-of-god.pdf

67. Dan Brown, *The Da Vinci Code* (Anchor, 2005), 233.

68. Melito of Sardis, *On the Passover*, Introduction, 8.

69. Justin Martyr, *First Apology*, 63.

70. Ignatius of Antioch, *Letter to the Romans*, 1.

71. Aristides, *The Apology of Aristides*, II.

72. Lucian of Samosata, *The Passing of Peregrinus*, 11-13.

73. Pliny the Younger, *Letter to Trajan*, Book X. Letter 96.

74. Ignatius of Antioch, *Letter to the Smyrnaeans*, 2.

75. "The symbol of Chalcedon" October 22, 451. Available online at: http://www.ccel.org/ccel/schaff/creeds2.iv.i.iii.html

## CHAPTER SIX

76. Dawkins, *The God Delusion*, 33-34.

77. Ibid, 34.

78. Dawkins, *The Selfish Gene*, (Oxford: Oxford University Press, 1989, first published in 1976), 36.

79. Frank Sheed, *Theology and Sanity* (San Francisco: Ignatius Press, 1993), 92.

80. Cited in Sheed, 97.

81. Translation from the *Christian Classics Ethereal Library*. Available online at: https://www.ccel.org/creeds/athanasian.creed.html

82. "Formula to adopt from now on in cases in which the Profession of Faith is prescribed by law in substitution of the Tridentine formula and the oath against modernism" Congregation for the Doctrine of the Faith, July 17, 1967. Available online at: http://www.vatican.va/roman_curia/congregations/cfaith/documents/rc_con_cfaith_doc_19670717_formula-professio-fidei_en.html

83. Augustine, *On the Trinity*, Book X. Chapter 9.

84. Augustine, *On the Trinity*, Book IX. Chapter 5.

85. Randall Harris, *The Contemporaries Meet the Classics on the Holy Spirit* (Howard Publishing: West Monroe, 2004), 68.

86. Cited in CCC 255.

87. Joseph Ratzinger. *Introduction to Christianity* (San Francisco: Ignatius Press, 1990), 183.

88. Ibid, 183.

# GLOSSARY

**ANSELM (1033 — 1103):** Monk, theologian, and Archbishop of Canterbury, he is known for his book *Proslogion*, which argues that reason requires men to believe in God, and *Cur Deus Homo*, which argues that Divine Love responding to human rebelliousness required that God should become a man.

**BEING:** existence as a unity or the fact that something "is." We know that God is "being itself" and because of this, there is only one God (Dt 6:4). Within creation there are many different things that have "being" and exist as unified entities, but have different natures or essences.

**CONTINGENT:** something that depends on another event, situation, or being; opposite of necessary

**EVIL:** absence of good or a corruption of a good thing that God created. Moral evil occurs when a rational being, such as a human, acts against the good. Physical evil is the corruption of good, created things by a natural disaster or occurrence.

**EXISTENTIALISM:** a philosophical theory or approach that emphasizes the existence of the individual person as a free and responsible agent determining his or her own development through acts of the will. Existentialism tends to be atheistic (although there is a strand of Christian existentialism deriving from the work of Kierkegaard), to disparage scientific knowledge, and to deny the existence of objective values, stressing instead the reality and significance of human freedom and experience.

**HOLY TRINITY:** One God (being itself) in three persons (Father, Son and Holy Spirit), all with one, divine nature.

HYPOSTATIC UNION: Prior to the incarnation, God the Son was one person (his person is the Son) with one nature (his nature is divine). Upon becoming incarnate, God the Son assumed a second nature, a human nature, as the man Jesus. However, nothing in the person or the divine nature of God the Son changed during this process. God the Son as one person now possesses two natures, one fully divine and the other fully human.

INCARNATION: The Son of God, the second person of the Trinity, assumed human nature and became man in order to accomplish our salvation. Jesus Christ, the Son of God, is both true God and true man, not part God and part man.

INFINITE: without end or limit. God is infinite because nothing limits him.

IPSUM ESSE: the "sheer act of being" or "being itself"

MIRACLE: when God intervenes in the world and causes an event to happen that has no natural explanation.

"MORALISTIC THERAPEUTIC DEISM": belief that God is simply a powerful being that created the world (deism), wants us to be good (moralistic), and exists to help us when we're in need (therapeutic).

NATURE: Nature refers to what someone or something is or its essence.

NECESSARY: something that depends on nothing else to exist; opposite of contingent

NON-COMPETITIVE CAUSALITY: In regards to humans, God does not negate our freedom but, in knowing what we will freely do, he is able to fold our free choices into his good, providential plan for his creation. God's providence does not compete with our freedom.

OMNIPOTENT: having complete or unlimited power

**OMNISCIENCE:** knowing every real of possible thing; having unlimited understanding or knowledge

**PANTHEISM:** the belief that every element of the universe is divine, and that divinity is equally present in everything.

**PERSON:** Person refers to someone in relationship with someone or something else (who someone is vis-à-vis another created thing).

**PROCESS THEOLOGY:** denies God has direct control over the world. Process theologians say God "persuades" rather than coerces his creation and so evil exists because such persuasion isn't 100% effective.

**PROOFS FOR GOD'S EXISTENCE:** converging and convincing arguments for the existence of God. These are "ways" or paths that lead to a knowledge of God, but not in the sense of "proofs" as in the natural sciences.

**PROVIDENCE:** how God orders natural causes toward divinely-chosen, good ends.

**SUMMA THEOLOGIAE:** St. Thomas Aquinas' guide to "theology for beginners" which contains five ways of coming to know that God exists (five "proofs").